cooking
desserts

cooking
desserts

MURDOCH BOOKS

contents

Shake off the slumber of winter and wake up the senses with the pretty colours, delicate textures and zesty flavours of spring. Let your taste buds blossom this season.

The abundance of fresh fruit available during the summer season is cause for celebration. Make the most of the delightful array of berries, stone fruits and tropical fruits.

Autumn signals the beginning of colder, shorter days, but perhaps more importantly it indicates the time to enjoy warm, sweet and sticky desserts.

The perfect remedy for a dark, cold winter is comfort food — discover the deep golden colours of this season as well as the wonderfully warm and indulgent tastes and textures.

a taste for all seasons

Many cookbooks explore exotic corners of the culinary world or delight in extending skills and knowledge. This book, however, has a very simple aim: to offer great desserts that work every time. The chosen recipes are not tricky or fancy; they are all reliable, a few even very simple, and many welcomingly familiar. Above all, they taste, smell and look wonderful. They are divided by season, with an emphasis on fresh, good-quality ingredients and classic dessert-making techniques. If you glance through the book's pages, moving from one season to another, you'll discover desserts so tempting that you will wish it was summer, autumn, winter and spring all at the same time so that you could delve into everything straight away. Even the names sound good — brown sugar cream pots with roasted plums in autumn, coconut, mango and almond tart in spring, mango and star anise sorbet for summer and decadent chocolate and cinnamon self-saucing puddings in winter.

Fruits feature in many recipes, and have been largely kept to their season — so you won't see fresh pears in a spring recipe or blueberries in the winter chapter. You will be well rewarded if you can wait for summer to arrive before indulging in strawberry and mascarpone mousse, or the onset of cold, short days to savour some pear and walnut frangipane tart. The basic building blocks of cakes, pastries and puddings — eggs, flour, sugar, butter, cream and vanilla — are common to all chapters and with them on hand you often only need to buy a few more ingredients and you are away. Add some fruit, chocolate, honey, nuts, liqueurs or spices such as cardamom and cinnamon for some truly memorable desserts.

A number of essential techniques are covered — classic procedures that you will come across time and time again, and so are good to master. These include how to make perfect shortcrust (pie) pastry, custard and glossy meringue. Some recipes are demanding, but that can be exactly what you're looking for every now and then. Try profiteroles with coffee mascarpone and dark chocolate sauce in spring or chocolate ganache log in autumn when you feel like a challenge. Many other recipes are almost suspiciously simple. Also, as with the ingredients, you may find that most of the necessary equipment is already in your kitchen, such as a food processor and blender, cake tins of various sizes, sieves, bowls, spoons and rolling pins.

Nothing will entice you more than the desserts themselves, which really need no introduction.

spring

Pretty colours and gentle flavours characterize the desserts in this chapter. For example, delicate panna cotta filo with rosewater syrup and pistachios, and cardamom kulfi could only be delightful spring treats. The dishes are not yet filled with the brilliance and boldness of summer flavours but at the same time are no longer dominated by the rich heaviness of winter ingredients. Many contain a bit of both — lime and coconut rice pudding, for example, retains the comforting texture of a winter dish but marks the new season with the clean taste of lime and even looks forward to the summer months with creamy tropical coconut.

As there should be when spring arrives, there is a lightness and freshness to these desserts. There is even an element of healthiness to them — but not too much! — with the clean, tart citrus flavours of limes and lemons, the slight sharpness of yoghurt and the tang of ginger to give things a little bite and wake up the taste buds. Refreshing granitas and gelatos in shades of ruby red and pale gold start to make an appearance, as do fruit-filled tarts and light pastries. Baked desserts like lemon tart and lemon, fig and walnut cake are a sure sign that afternoons can be reclaimed from the slumber of winter.

Chocolate and alcohol don't feature highly, but lest you fear a too-healthy shock to the system, there are still desserts with a good dash of cream of one sort or another in them — chocolate almondine semifreddo is nothing if not indulgent — and there are a few desserts that keep chocolate close by, as a sauce that you can add as generously as you like.

Of the classic techniques introduced in this chapter, perhaps the most difficult would be making perfectly smooth custard for the coconut and ginger crème brûlée. The trick is to ensure that the water in the bain-marie does not bubble or bubbles will form in the custard. This is more of a concern when making crème caramel, as you can see the bubbles in the custard when you turn it out, but it is still worth getting the technique right when making a crème brûlée. On the other hand, no one is going to turn away a rich, gooey custard just because of a few bubbles, so relax.

coconut and ginger
crème brûlée .... serves 4

THIS TRADITIONAL BAKED EGG CUSTARD IS GIVEN A TOUCH OF THE TROPICAL THROUGH THE ADDITION OF GINGER AND COCONUT — ALL THE MORE PLEASANT BECAUSE THEIR SHARP, FRESH FLAVOURS ARE UNEXPECTED. DON'T RUSH THIS RECIPE — IT'S NOT COMPLICATED BUT EACH STEP NEEDS TO BE FOLLOWED WITH CARE.

thickened (whipping) cream	500 ml (17 fl oz/2 cups)
shredded coconut	20 g (3/4 oz/1/3 cup)
fresh ginger	3 teaspoons finely grated
egg yolks	4, at room temperature
caster (superfine) sugar	55 g (2 oz/1/4 cup)
raw (demerara) sugar	2 tablespoons

Preheat the oven to 160°C (315°F/Gas 2–3).

Put the cream, shredded coconut and ginger into a saucepan. Slowly heat the mixture, stirring, until it is just below boiling point. Strain into a bowl, discarding the coconut and ginger.

Whisk the egg yolks and caster sugar in a heatproof bowl until thick and pale. This will take about 5 minutes with an electric whisk. Gradually whisk in the hot cream. Place the bowl over a saucepan of barely simmering water, making sure the base of the bowl doesn't touch the water. Stir the mixture over the simmering water for 10 minutes, or until it has thickened slightly and coats the back of a spoon.

Put 4 x 125 ml (4 fl oz/1/2 cup) capacity ovenproof dishes in a roasting tin and divide the cream mixture among the dishes. Add enough boiling water to the roasting tin to come three-quarters of the way up the side of the dishes. Bake for 20–25 minutes, or until the custards are just set. Carefully remove the dishes from the water and set aside to cool to room temperature, then cover and refrigerate the custards for 3 hours.

Preheat the grill (broiler) to high. Put the custards in a shallow roasting tin and surround them with ice cubes. Sprinkle the tops of the custards with the raw sugar. Place under the hot grill until the sugar has melted and turned golden brown. Alternatively, use a small blow torch to caramelize the sugar.

Gradually whisk the hot cream into the egg yolk mixture.

The custard must be thick enough to coat the back of the spoon.

ruby red grapefruit grapefruit granita

.... serves 4–6

GRANITA CAN BE MADE FROM ANY CITRUS FRUIT — LEMON IS THE CLASSIC CHOICE, BUT GRAPEFRUIT, ORANGE AND LIME CAN ALL BE USED SUCCESSFULLY. TANGY AND SMOOTH AT THE SAME TIME, THIS PRETTY RUBY RED VERSION LITERALLY MELTS IN THE MOUTH. YOU WILL NEED ABOUT THREE GRAPEFRUIT FOR THIS RECIPE.

sugar	110 g (3¾ oz/½ cup)
freshly squeezed ruby grapefruit juice	350 ml (12 fl oz)
orange muscat dessert wine	150 ml (5 fl oz)

Put the sugar and 125 ml (4 fl oz/½ cup) of water in a small saucepan and bring to the boil. Reduce the heat and simmer for 3–4 minutes, then remove from the heat and set aside to cool.

Combine the grapefruit juice, wine and cooled sugar syrup in a shallow freezer-proof tray and freeze for 2 hours, or until the mixture has started to freeze around the edges. Break up the mixture with a fork, then return it to the freezer and repeat the process every 30 minutes until the granita has frozen and has a rough, icy texture.

Grapefruit arrived relatively recently on the culinary scene, first introduced into North America from the Bahamas in the early nineteenth century. Today, they are available with or without seeds, and in a range of colours, from yellow to pink to ruby red. The original yellow-fleshed fruit is a favourite for breakfast; eaten fresh, with maybe just a sprinkling of sugar, it makes a fairly bracing start to the day. The pinker varieties are generally sweeter. Grapefruit go well with cheese, pears and certain nuts, make good marmalade and are delicious in chicken and prawn (shrimp) salads, fruit salads, sorbets and granitas. Choose heavy fruit with unblemished skin.

panna cotta filo with rosewater syrup and pistachios............serves 6

THIS RECIPE SEEMS COMPLICATED, BUT ONCE THE PANNA COTTA IS MADE AND SAFELY IN THE REFRIGERATOR, IT'S ALL SMOOTH SAILING. TAKE CARE TO ADD ONLY THE SPECIFIED AMOUNT OF ROSEWATER AS IT CAN BE SURPRISINGLY STRONG — TOO MUCH AND THE SYRUP WILL BE SICKLY SWEET.

panna cotta

gelatine sheet	1 x 6 g (1/8 oz)
	(or 1 1/2 teaspoons powdered gelatine)
cream (whipping)	500 ml (17 fl oz/2 cups)
plain yoghurt	250 g (9 oz/1 cup)
caster (superfine) sugar	150 g (5 1/2 oz/2/3 cup)
vanilla bean	1

filo shells

filo pastry	4 sheets
unsalted butter	40 g (1 1/2 oz), melted
caster (superfine) sugar	2 tablespoons

rosewater syrup

caster (superfine) sugar	115 g (4 oz/1/2 cup)
cinnamon stick	1
rosewater	1/2 teaspoon
rose pink food colouring	1 drop, optional
roasted pistachio nuts	2 tablespoons, chopped

To make the panna cotta, either soak the gelatine sheet in cold water for 5 minutes, or until soft, or put 2 tablespoons of water in a small bowl, sprinkle with the powdered gelatine and set aside for 2 minutes to sponge and swell. Put the cream, yoghurt and sugar in a saucepan. Spilt the vanilla bean lengthways and scrape the seeds into the saucepan, discarding the pod. Stir the mixture over low heat until the sugar has dissolved. Drain the gelatine sheet and squeeze out the excess water. Add the gelatine sheet or the sponged gelatine to the saucepan and stir until the gelatine has dissolved. Pour the mixture into 6 x 125 ml (4 fl oz/1/2 cup) moulds. Refrigerate for 5 hours, or until set.

Meanwhile, preheat the oven to 190°C (375°F/Gas 5). Lightly brush a sheet of filo pastry with the melted butter. Sprinkle one-third of the sugar over the pastry, top with another sheet of pastry and press down gently to stick the pastry together. Repeat this process until there are four layers of pastry. Using a sharp knife, cut 6 x 12 cm (4 1/2 inch) square pieces from the pastry. Line a 6-hole giant muffin tin with the pastry squares. Line each pastry shell with a square of baking paper and weigh it down with baking beads or uncooked rice. Bake for 2 minutes, then remove the paper and beads and bake for a further 2–3 minutes, or until lightly golden. Cool the pastry shells on a wire rack.

To make the rosewater syrup, put 160 ml (5 1/4 fl oz) of water, the sugar and cinnamon stick in a small saucepan. Stir over low heat until the sugar has dissolved. Increase the heat to high and simmer for 3–4 minutes, or until the mixture is slightly syrupy. Add the rosewater and food colouring, if using. Remove from the heat and set aside to cool. Remove the cinnamon stick.

Run a spatula or blunt knife around the panna cotta, then carefully invert them into the pastry shells. Drizzle the panna cotta with the rosewater syrup and sprinkle with the pistachios.

Make sure you use a muffin tin with large holes.

Simmer the rosewater syrup until it is slightly syrupy.

cardamom kulfi .... serves 8

THIS SIMPLE, ELEGANT ICE CREAM FROM INDIA IS MADE BY BOILING MILK UNTIL IT REDUCES AND CONDENSES, THEN FLAVOURING IT WITH INGREDIENTS SUCH AS PISTACHIO NUTS, CARDAMOM AND ROSEWATER. TO TURN OUT THE KULFI, BRIEFLY DIP THE MOULDS IN VERY HOT WATER, THEN INVERT THEM ONTO SERVING PLATES.

pistachio nuts	40 g (1 1/2 oz/1/4 cup)
milk	1.5 litres (52 fl oz/6 cups)
cardamom pods	21
caster (superfine) sugar	115 g (4 oz/1/2 cup)
lime zest	1/2 teaspoon finely grated

Preheat the grill (broiler) to medium. Spread the pistachios on a baking tray and place under the grill for about 3 minutes, or until aromatic and lightly toasted. Set aside to cool slightly, then roughly chop the nuts.

Put the milk and 9 of the cardamom pods in a large heavy-based saucepan. Bring to the boil, making sure that the milk doesn't boil over. Reduce the heat and simmer for 15–20 minutes, or until the liquid has reduced by one-third. Strain the mixture into a container suitable for freezing. Add the sugar and stir until it has dissolved. Stir in half the chopped pistachios and the grated lime zest. Set aside to cool for 30 minutes. Store the remaining pistachios in an airtight container.

Freeze the kulfi until almost firm, stirring every 30 minutes. (This can take from 3 to 6 hours, depending on the freezer.) Rinse 8 x 170 ml (5 1/2 fl oz/2/3 cup) dariole moulds with cold water and shake out the excess. Pack the kulfi into the moulds and freeze until completely firm.

Remove the moulds from the freezer 5 minutes before serving. Turn the kulfi out onto serving plates and sprinkle the reserved pistachios over the top. Lightly crush the remaining cardamom pods to release some of the seeds. Sprinkle a few seeds on top of the kulfi and sprinkle the pods around the base.

Strain the milk to remove the cardamom pods.

Add half the chopped pistachios and all the grated lime zest.

Once the kulfi is almost firm, pack it into dariole moulds.

banana and pineapple
tortilla fingers . . . . serves 6

BANANA FRITTERS ARE COMMONLY MADE WITH BATTER, DEEP-FRIED AND THEN SERVED PIPING HOT WITH ICE CREAM OR COCONUT CREAM. THIS VERSION MAKES LIFE EASY BY USING TORTILLAS AND GRILLING (BROILING), RATHER THAN FRYING THE FRITTERS, WHILE THE PINEAPPLE ADDS A JUICY, SWEET, CARAMELIZED FLAVOUR.

fresh pineapple	4 thin slices
white wheat flour tortillas	4 large
bananas	2
unsalted butter	40 g (1 1/2 oz), melted
soft brown sugar	2 tablespoons
icing (confectioners') sugar	for dusting

coconut yoghurt

Greek-style yoghurt	125 g (4 1/2 oz/1/2 cup)
soft brown sugar	2 tablespoons
shredded coconut	2 tablespoons
lemon zest	2 teaspoons finely grated
lemon juice	1 teaspoon

Preheat the grill (broiler) to high. Cut each pineapple slice into thirds and remove the hard core. Grill (broil) the pineapple for 8 minutes each side, or until just starting to brown. Remove and set aside to cool.

To make the coconut yoghurt, put the yoghurt, brown sugar, shredded coconut, lemon zest and lemon juice in a small bowl and stir to combine. Refrigerate until needed.

Cut the tortillas into three even strips about 5 cm (2 inches) wide. Peel the bananas and cut them in half lengthways and then into pieces slightly longer than the width of the tortilla strips. Roll the banana pieces in half of the melted butter and sprinkle with the brown sugar. Place a piece of pineapple widthways across the centre of each tortilla strip and top with a piece of banana. Fold the tortilla over the banana, roll up and place on a baking tray, seam side down. Brush the tortillas with the remaining melted butter.

Preheat the grill to high. Grill the tortilla fingers for 8–10 minutes, or until golden brown, then turn and cook until browned all over. Dust with icing sugar and serve with the coconut yoghurt.

Cut each of the tortillas into three even strips.

Place the pineapple and banana widthways across the tortillas.

Carefully roll up the tortillas to enclose the filling.

white chocolate mousse
with almond tuiles . . . . serves 6

TRYING A NEW RECIPE CAN BE REWARDING, AND IT'S PERHAPS NORMAL THAT WE SET CULINARY CHALLENGES FOR OURSELVES PRECISELY WHEN WE SHOULDN'T — THAT IS, WHEN GUESTS ARE COMING FOR DINNER. THIS DESSERT IS A GOOD CHOICE FOR SUCH OCCASIONS AS IT NOT ONLY LOOKS IMPRESSIVE, BUT ALSO CAN BE MADE IN ADVANCE.

egg yolks	6, at room temperature
caster (superfine) sugar	55 g (2 oz/$\frac{1}{4}$ cup)
milk	375 ml (13 fl oz/1$\frac{1}{2}$ cups)
white chocolate chips	225 g (8 oz/1$\frac{1}{4}$ cups)
cognac	80 ml (2$\frac{1}{2}$ fl oz/$\frac{1}{3}$ cup)
powdered gelatine	2 teaspoons
cream (whipping)	455 ml (16 fl oz)

almond tuiles

liquid glucose	1 tablespoon
unsalted butter	30 g (1 oz)
raw caster (superfine) sugar	1$\frac{1}{2}$ tablespoons
plain (all-purpose) flour	2 tablespoons
blanched almonds	30 g (1 oz/scant $\frac{1}{4}$ cup) finely chopped

Beat the egg yolks and caster sugar in a bowl until smooth and pale. This will take about 5 minutes with an electric whisk. Pour the milk into a saucepan and heat until it is just below boiling point. Whisk the hot milk into the egg yolk mixture, then return the mixture to the saucepan. Cook over low heat, stirring constantly, for about 2 minutes, or until the mixture is thick enough to coat the back of a spoon. Do not allow the mixture to boil or it will separate.

Strain the mixture into a bowl, add the white chocolate chips and stir until the chocolate has melted. Stir in the cognac. Put 1$\frac{1}{2}$ tablespoons of water in a small bowl and sprinkle with the gelatine. Leave the gelatine to sponge and swell. Stir the gelatine mixture into the chocolate mixture and set aside to cool for at least 1 hour.

Whip the cream until soft peaks form. Using a metal spoon, fold a large scoop of cream into the chocolate mixture, then gently fold in the remaining cream. Divide the mixture among 6 x 185 ml (6 fl oz/$\frac{3}{4}$ cup) glasses and refrigerate until set.

Meanwhile, to make the almond tuiles, preheat the oven to 180°C (350°F/Gas 4). Line a baking tray with baking paper. Put the glucose, butter and sugar in a saucepan and cook over low heat, stirring until melted. Increase the heat and bring to the boil. Immediately remove the saucepan from the heat and stir in the flour and almonds.

Using half the mixture, spoon teaspoons of the mixture onto the prepared tray, allowing for spreading. Bake for 4–5 minutes, or until golden brown. Set aside to cool for 15–20 seconds, then, using a spatula and working quickly, lift the biscuits and drape them over a rolling pin or the handle of a wooden spoon. They will quickly set in a curved shape. Repeat with the remaining mixture. Store the tuiles in an airtight container until ready to serve.

Serve the mousse with the almond tuiles.

lime and coconut
rice puddings . . . . serves 4

IT'S NO ACCIDENT THAT LIMES AND COCONUTS GROW IN SIMILAR PARTS OF THE WORLD: THEIR FLAVOURS COMPLEMENT EACH OTHER PERFECTLY. THE SHARPNESS OF LIME MEANS IT IS OFTEN USED AS A FLAVOUR ENHANCER, AND HERE IT NICELY CUTS THROUGH THE RICHNESS OF THE COCONUT CREAM.

milk	200 ml (7 fl oz)
coconut cream	800 ml (28 fl oz)
lime	1, zest finely grated
lime juice	60 ml (2 fl oz/$1/4$ cup)
makrut (kaffir lime) leaves	3, halved
medium-grain rice	140 g (5 oz/$2/3$ cup)
palm sugar (jaggery)	100 g ($3^1/2$ oz/$3/4$ cup) shaved or 100 g ($3^1/2$ oz/$1/2$ cup) soft brown sugar
toasted shredded coconut	for decoration, optional

Put the milk, coconut cream, lime zest, lime juice and lime leaves in a large saucepan and bring to the boil. Add the rice and stir to combine. Reduce the heat to low and simmer, stirring occasionally, for 25–30 minutes, or until the rice is tender.

Remove the saucepan from the heat and add the palm sugar, stirring until it has dissolved and the mixture is creamy.

Remove the lime leaves and divide the rice pudding among 4 x 250 ml (9 fl oz/1 cup) capacity heatproof glasses or ramekins. Serve warm or cold, decorated with shredded coconut, if using.

The coconut tree and its fruit have been appreciated for centuries. Its uses range from supplying material for thatching and weaving to providing a nutritious and refreshing drink — complete with its own cup. When not quite ripe, coconut flesh is soft and jelly-like and the juice sweet and watery. As the coconut ripens, the flesh hardens and the amount of juice decreases. This juice is quite different from coconut milk and cream, which are produced by soaking grated coconut flesh in boiling water and squeezing out the resulting liquid. Other products include copra, which is dried coconut flesh; coconut oil, which is made from copra; desiccated coconut; and coconut liqueur.

three ways with garnishes

hazelnut and vanilla praline

Coarsely chop 70 g (2½ oz/½ cup) roasted skinned hazelnuts and spread the nuts on a baking tray lined with baking paper. Put 225 g (8 oz/1 cup) caster (superfine) sugar and 125 ml (4 fl oz/½ cup) water into a small saucepan. Split a vanilla bean in half lengthways and scrape the seeds into the saucepan, discarding the pod. Cook over low heat, stirring until the sugar has dissolved. Bring to the boil and, without stirring, cook for 5 minutes, or until the mixture turns a deep golden colour. Pour the mixture over the hazelnuts and leave to set for 15 minutes. Break up the praline with your hands or crush it in a food processor and sprinkle it over ice cream or stir it into lightly whipped cream. Makes about 225 g (8 oz).

candied walnuts

Preheat the oven to 180°C (350°F/Gas 4). Combine 100 g (3½ oz/1 cup) roasted walnut halves, 2 tablespoons raw (demerara) sugar and 2 tablespoons corn syrup in a bowl. Spread the mixture onto a baking tray lined with baking paper and bake for 5 minutes. Remove from the oven and toss to mix everything well. Return to the oven and bake for a further 5 minutes. Leave the walnuts to cool on the tray, then remove them with a spatula. Use the walnuts in biscuit dough, to decorate cakes and tarts, or stir them into softened vanilla ice cream and freeze until firm. Makes 200 g (7 oz/1 cup).

coconut tuiles

Preheat the oven to 180°C (350°F/Gas 4). Combine 55 g (2 oz/¼ cup) caster (superfine) sugar, 30 g (1 oz/⅓ cup) desiccated coconut and 2 teaspoons plain (all-purpose) flour in a bowl. Add 1 lightly beaten egg white and 10 g (¼ oz) melted unsalted butter and stir to combine. Drop ½ teaspoon of the mixture onto a baking tray lined with baking paper. Using the back of a teaspoon dipped in water, spread out the mixture to a very thin 10 cm (4 inch) circle, leaving 5 cm (2 inches) between each tuile. Repeat with the remaining mixture. Bake for 5 minutes, or until light golden. Leave the biscuits on the trays to cool. These tuiles are great as a garnish for cold puddings and ice cream. Makes 20.

hazelnut and vanilla praline

coconut, mango and almond tart
.... serves 6–8

WHEN YOU HAVE A LOVELY, RIPE MANGO TO HAND IT'S HARD NOT TO JUST EAT IT RIGHT THERE AND THEN AND HANG THE DESSERT. BUT MANGO AND ALMONDS IN BUTTERY PASTRY IS A CLASSIC COMBINATION, AND WORTH THE TEMPORARY EFFORT OF SELF-RESTRAINT. THE ALMOND PASTRY SHOULD BE CHILLED WELL BEFORE USING.

pastry

plain (all-purpose) flour	210 g (7$\frac{1}{2}$ oz/1$\frac{2}{3}$ cups)
raw caster (superfine) sugar	60 g (2$\frac{1}{4}$ oz/$\frac{1}{4}$ cup)
ground almonds	25 g (1 oz/$\frac{1}{4}$ cup)
unsalted butter	150 g (5$\frac{1}{2}$ oz), chilled and cubed
egg yolks	2, at room temperature
iced water	1–2 tablespoons

filling

unsalted butter	185 g (6$\frac{1}{2}$ oz), softened
raw caster (superfine) sugar	185 g (6$\frac{1}{2}$ oz/heaped $\frac{3}{4}$ cup)
eggs	2, at room temperature
ground almonds	70 g (2$\frac{1}{2}$ oz/$\frac{2}{3}$ cup)
plain (all-purpose) flour	60 g (2$\frac{1}{4}$ oz/$\frac{1}{2}$ cup)
desiccated coconut	90 g (3$\frac{1}{4}$ oz/1 cup)
coconut cream	2 tablespoons
coconut liqueur	1 tablespoon
mango	1
flaked coconut	30 g (1 oz/$\frac{1}{2}$ cup)
vanilla ice cream or	
whipped cream	to serve

To make the pastry, put the flour, sugar, ground almonds and butter in a food processor. Process until the mixture resembles fine crumbs. Add the egg yolks and process until smooth. Add the water, $\frac{1}{2}$ teaspoon at a time, until the dough clumps together in a ball. Flatten the dough to a rough rectangle, cover with plastic wrap and refrigerate for 30 minutes.

Preheat the oven to 190°C (375°F/Gas 5). Grease a 19 x 27 cm (7$\frac{1}{2}$ x 10$\frac{3}{4}$ inch) loose-based tart tin.

To make the filling, cream the butter and sugar with electric beaters for about 3 minutes. Add the eggs, one at a time, beating well after each addition. Fold in the ground almonds, flour and desiccated coconut. Lightly stir in the coconut cream and coconut liqueur.

Roll out the pastry on a sheet of baking paper to cover the base and side of the tin. Place the pastry in the tin and trim any excess. Line the pastry with a sheet of crumpled baking paper and pour in some baking beads or uncooked rice. Bake for 10 minutes, remove the paper and beads and bake for another 5 minutes. Reduce the oven to 170°C (325°F/Gas 3).

Cut the cheeks from the mango, peel them and cut each into 3 mm ($\frac{1}{8}$ inch) thick slices. Spread the filling in the pastry case and arrange the mango slices in two rows down the length of the filling. Scatter the flaked coconut over the top and press it into the exposed filling with your fingertips, giving an uneven surface. Bake for 30 minutes, or until the coconut begins to brown, then cover loosely with foil. Bake for another 35 minutes, or until the filling is set and the top is golden brown. Serve warm with vanilla ice cream or serve cold with lightly whipped cream.

Arrange the mango slices in two rows over the filling.

The flaked coconut doesn't have to be arranged neatly.

ginger and grapefruit puddings with mascarpone cream
. . . . serves 6

THESE PUDDINGS ARE IDEAL FOR SPRING, WHEN ANYTHING TOO HEAVY OR RICH DOESN'T FEEL RIGHT. THEY HAVE A LIGHT, CLEAN FLAVOUR DUE TO THE GINGER AND RUBY GRAPEFRUIT, WHICH IS MATCHED BY A FLUFFY, WARM SPONGE. OF COURSE, IF THAT SOUNDS TOO HEALTHY, YOU CAN ADD A GOOD DOLLOP OF MASCARPONE CREAM.

ruby grapefruit	1 large
stem ginger in syrup	40 g (1 1/2 oz/1/3 cup) drained, plus 3 teaspoons syrup
golden syrup or dark corn syrup	1 1/2 tablespoons
unsalted butter	125 g (4 1/2 oz), softened
caster (superfine) sugar	115 g (4 oz/1/2 cup)
eggs	2, at room temperature
self-raising flour	185 g (6 1/2 oz/1 1/2 cups)
ground ginger	1 teaspoon
milk	80 ml (2 1/2 fl oz/1/3 cup)

mascarpone cream

mascarpone cheese	125 g (4 1/2 oz/heaped 1/2 cup)
cream (whipping)	125 ml (4 fl oz/1/2 cup)
icing (confectioners') sugar	1 tablespoon, sifted

Preheat the oven to 170°C (325°F/Gas 3). Grease 6 x 170 ml (5 1/2 fl oz/2/3 cup) pudding moulds or ramekins.

Finely grate 2 teaspoons of zest from the ruby grapefruit and set aside. Slice the grapefruit around its circumference, one-third of the way down. Peel the larger piece of grapefruit, removing any white pith, and cut the flesh into six 1 cm (1/2 inch) slices. Squeeze 3 teaspoons of juice from the remaining grapefruit. Finely chop the stem ginger.

Combine the grapefruit juice, ginger syrup and golden or corn syrup in a small bowl. Divide the mixture among the pudding moulds and top with a slice of grapefruit, trimming to fit.

Put the butter and sugar in a bowl and beat with electric beaters until pale and smooth. Beat in the eggs, one at a time. Sift in the flour and ground ginger, add the grapefruit zest, chopped ginger and milk and mix well. Divide the mixture among the moulds.

Cover each mould with foil and put them in a deep roasting tin. Pour in enough boiling water to come halfway up the side of the moulds. Cover the roasting tin with foil, sealing the edges well. Bake the puddings for 30–35 minutes, or until set.

To make the mascarpone cream, mix the mascarpone, cream and icing sugar in a small bowl until smooth.

To serve, gently invert the puddings onto serving plates and serve with the mascarpone cream.

The grapefruit syrup gives the puddings a lovely moist top.

Use scissors to trim the grapefruit to fit the moulds.

limoncello syllabub . . . . serves 6

THIS ELEGANT DESSERT HAS ITS ORIGINS IN THE BRITISH COUNTRYSIDE OF THE SEVENTEENTH CENTURY, THOUGH THE ADDITION OF LIMONCELLO GIVES THE SYLLABUB A DEFINITE FEELING OF SOUTHERN ITALY. DON'T OMIT THE ALMOND TUILE BISCUITS, AS THEY PROVIDE A CRISP CONTRAST TO THE SYLLABUB'S LIGHT AND CREAMY TEXTURE.

limoncello	125 ml (4 fl oz/1/2 cup)
caster (superfine) sugar	115 g (4 oz/1/2 cup)
lemon zest	1 teaspoon finely grated
lemon juice	60 ml (2 fl oz/1/4 cup)
vanilla bean	1
cream (whipping)	250 ml (9 fl oz/1 cup)
almond tuile biscuits	to serve (page 23)

Put the limoncello in a non-metallic mixing bowl with the sugar, lemon zest and lemon juice. Split the vanilla bean in half lengthways and scrape the seeds into the bowl, discarding the pod. Stir to combine. Set aside for 2 hours, stirring occasionally to dissolve the sugar.

Beat the cream with electric beaters until very stiff peaks form. Gently fold in the limoncello mixture, 2 tablespoons at a time. Divide the syllabub among 6 glasses and refrigerate for 5 hours. Serve accompanied by almond tuile biscuits.

This refreshing bittersweet lemon liqueur has been popular for centuries. Originally a regional drink from southern Italy, limoncello can be made at home without great difficulty, requiring only lemons, wholegrain alcohol, sugar and water. For devotees, however, the best is still made in its traditional homes of Capri and the Italian Amalfi coast. It is said that the local lemons there cannot be beaten for taste and aroma — and perhaps, with that special blend of sun, sea, summer and Italian charm, they are different to lemons grown elsewhere. Limoncello is always drunk cold, and makes an excellent digestif; it is also served over ice cream or fruit salads.

lime and ricotta pudding .... serves 4

THIS REFRESHING PUDDING COULDN'T BE EASIER TO MAKE, AND APART FROM THE LIME AND FRESH RICOTTA, YOU MAY ALREADY HAVE ALL THE INGREDIENTS TO HAND. THE QUALITY OF THE RICOTTA IS IMPORTANT — IT SHOULD BE CRUMBLY, MOIST AND FRESH-TASTING, NOT BLAND AND DULL.

unsalted butter	60 g (2¼ oz), softened
caster (superfine) sugar	350 g (12 oz/1½ cups)
lime zest	2 teaspoons finely grated
eggs	3, at room temperature, separated
fresh ricotta cheese or good-quality tub of ricotta	375 g (13 oz/1½ cups)
self-raising flour	30 g (1 oz/¼ cup)
lime juice	60 ml (2 fl oz/¼ cup)
icing (confectioners') sugar	2 teaspoons

Preheat the oven to 180°C (350°F/Gas 4) and grease a 1.5 litre (52 fl oz/6 cup) capacity ovenproof dish.

Using electric beaters, beat the butter and caster sugar with half the lime zest for 30 seconds, or until combined. Add the egg yolks, one at a time, and beat until well combined. Gradually add the ricotta and flour alternately and beat until the mixture is thick and smooth. Stir in the lime juice.

Beat the egg whites until stiff peaks form and gently fold into the ricotta mixture in two batches. Pour the mixture into the prepared dish and place in a roasting tin. Pour enough hot water into the tin to come halfway up the sides of the dish. Bake for 1 hour.

Sift the icing sugar over the warm pudding and sprinkle with the remaining lime zest. Serve warm.

Alternately add spoonfuls of ricotta and spoonfuls of flour.

Make sure the mixture is thick and smooth.

Don't knock out the air when folding in the egg whites.

honeycomb and mascarpone cheesecake with white chocolate sauce .... serves 8

THIS INDULGENT VARIATION ON THE CLASSIC CHEESECAKE FEATURES CREAM, MASCARPONE CHEESE AND CHOCOLATE HONEYCOMB TO ENSURE A REALLY CREAMY, RICH RESULT. AND TO TOP IT OFF —— A SMOOTH AND DECADENT WHITE CHOCOLATE SAUCE.

wholemeal biscuits (graham crackers)	100 g (3½ oz)
unsalted butter	70 g (2½ oz), melted
gelatine sheet	1 x 6 g (⅛ oz) (or 1½ teaspoons powdered gelatine)
thickened (whipping) cream	300 ml (10½ fl oz)
eggs	2, at room temperature, separated
mascarpone cheese	225 g (8 oz/1 cup)
caster (superfine) sugar	80 g (2¾ oz/⅓ cup)
natural vanilla extract	1 teaspoon
chocolate honeycomb bar	50 g (1¾ oz), crushed

white chocolate sauce

good-quality white chocolate	125 g (4½ oz/heaped ¾ cup) chopped
cream (whipping)	80 ml (2½ fl oz/⅓ cup)

Lightly grease the base of a 20 cm (8 inch) spring-form cake tin.

Put the biscuits in a food processor and process until they resemble fine crumbs. Put the melted butter in a small bowl, add the biscuit crumbs and stir to combine. Press the mixture into the base of the cake tin. Refrigerate for 15 minutes.

Either soak the gelatine sheet in cold water for 5 minutes, or until soft, or put 2 tablespoons of water in a small bowl, sprinkle with the powdered gelatine and set aside for 2 minutes to sponge and swell. Meanwhile, heat the cream in a small saucepan until it reaches simmering point. Remove the saucepan from the heat. Drain the gelatine sheet and squeeze out the excess water. Add the gelatine sheet or the sponged gelatine to the saucepan and stir until the gelatine has dissolved. Set aside to cool.

Beat the egg yolks, mascarpone, 55 g (2 oz/¼ cup) of the sugar and the vanilla in a small bowl with electric beaters until smooth. Fold in the crushed honeycomb bar. Add the cream mixture and mix well.

Beat the egg whites and remaining sugar until stiff peaks form. Fold into the mascarpone mixture with a metal spoon, then pour into the tin over the base and refrigerate overnight.

To make the white chocolate sauce, put the white chocolate and cream in a small heatproof bowl and place over a small saucepan of simmering water, making sure the base of the bowl doesn't touch the water. Stir until melted and smooth, then set aside to cool slightly.

To serve, cut the cheesecake into slices and drizzle with the white chocolate sauce.

Gently fold in the egg whites using a metal spoon.

Melt the chocolate over gentle heat so it doesn't burn.

the perfect ice cream

It is hard to match the rich creaminess of vanilla ice cream. The best flavour comes from infusing a silky egg custard with vanilla beans, while the perfect texture is achieved by churning or whisking the mixture as it freezes to break up the ice crystals. Ice-cream machines do the churning for you, but the hand-made method gives equally good results.

Whisk 5 egg yolks and 125 g (4½ oz/heaped ½ cup) caster (superfine) sugar with electric beaters for 3 minutes, or until pale and foamy. Put 300 ml (10½ fl oz) each of cream (whipping) and milk in a heavy-based saucepan. Roll 2 vanilla beans in your hands for 10 seconds, split lengthways and add them to the saucepan. Bring the mixture to a low simmer over medium heat, then remove from the heat. Whisk a little of the mixture into the egg mixture. Remove the vanilla beans and set aside. Pour the remaining cream mixture into the egg mixture, whisking constantly. Return the mixture to the clean saucepan. Cook over medium–low heat, stirring constantly with a wooden spoon, until the custard thickens enough to coat the back of a spoon. Do not allow it to boil or it will separate. Strain into a shallow container. Scrape the seeds from the vanilla beans and stir into the custard. Set aside to cool, then refrigerate until chilled.

If using an ice-cream machine, pour in the custard and follow the manufacturer's instructions. Alternatively, transfer the custard to the freezer. When the edges begin to freeze, whisk vigorously, then return to the freezer until partially frozen. Whisk again, then return to the freezer. When the custard is just frozen, whisk again. Repeat once more, or until the custard is smooth, thick and free of ice crystals. Freeze overnight. Use within 3 days. Serves 4.

lemon tart .... serves 6–8

THIS IS PERHAPS THE CLASSIC SPRINGTIME RECIPE. SERVE IT AT ANY TIME OF THE DAY — TO COMPLETE A SPECIAL LUNCH OR DINNER, OR EVEN FOR MORNING OR AFTERNOON TEA. THE FILLING IS NOT DIFFICULT TO MAKE, SO YOU CAN CONCENTRATE ON PERFECTING YOUR PASTRY-MAKING TECHNIQUES.

pastry

plain (all-purpose) flour	185 g (6¹/₂ oz/1¹/₂ cups)
icing (confectioners') sugar	60 g (2¹/₄ oz/¹/₂ cup)
ground almonds	35 g (1¹/₄ oz/¹/₃ cup)
unsalted butter	125 g (4¹/₂ oz), chilled and cubed
egg yolk	1, at room temperature

filling

lemon zest	1¹/₂ tablespoons finely grated
lemon juice	80 ml (2¹/₂ fl oz/¹/₃ cup), strained
eggs	5, at room temperature
caster (superfine) sugar	175 g (6 oz/³/₄ cup)
thickened (whipping) cream	300 ml (10¹/₂ fl oz)
icing (confectioners') sugar	for dusting
thick (double/heavy) cream	to serve

To make the pastry, put the flour, icing sugar, ground almonds and butter in a food processor and process until the mixture resembles fine crumbs. Add the egg yolk and process until the dough just comes together. Knead gently and briefly on a lightly floured surface until the dough is smooth. Form into a ball, flatten into a disc, cover with plastic wrap and refrigerate for 30 minutes.

Preheat the oven to 180°C (350°F/Gas 4) and grease a 22 cm (8¹/₂ inch) loose-based tart tin. Roll out the pastry between two sheets of baking paper to a thickness of 3 mm (¹/₈ inch) to cover the base and side of the tart tin. Peel off the top sheet of baking paper, carefully invert the pastry into the tin and peel off the second sheet of paper. Press the pastry gently into the base and side, ensuring the pastry is level with the top of the tin. Trim off any excess pastry. Refrigerate for 10 minutes.

Line the pastry with a sheet of crumpled baking paper and pour in some baking beads or uncooked rice. Place the tin on a baking tray and bake for 10 minutes. Remove the paper and beads and return to the oven for another 10–15 minutes, or until light golden. Set aside to cool. Reduce the oven to 140°C (275°F/Gas 1).

To make the filling, put the lemon zest, lemon juice, eggs, sugar and cream in a bowl and whisk until combined. Set aside for 10 minutes to allow the lemon zest to infuse the mixture, then strain the mixture. Carefully pour the filling into the pastry shell and bake for 45–50 minutes, or until just set. Set aside to cool for 10 minutes, then refrigerate until cold.

Dust the tart with icing sugar and serve with thick cream.

Use the baking paper to help transfer the pastry into the tin.

Lining the paper with baking beads stops the pastry bubbling.

chocolate almondine semifreddo . . . . serves 6

LITERALLY MEANING 'HALF-COLD' IN ITALIAN, A SEMIFREDDO IS A CHILLED OR PARTLY FROZEN ICE CREAM-STYLE DESSERT. IT IS EASIER TO MAKE THAN ICE CREAM, HOWEVER, AS THERE IS NO NEED TO CHURN OR WHISK THE FROZEN MIXTURE. THE SEMIFREDDO IS BEST EATEN WITHIN 4 TO 5 DAYS.

caster (superfine) sugar	80 g (2¾ oz/⅓ cup)
almonds	80 g (2¾ oz/½ cup)
cream (whipping)	600 ml (21 fl oz)
eggs	2, at room temperature, separated
icing (confectioners') sugar	125 g (4½ oz/1 cup)
cocoa powder	50 g (1¾ oz/heaped ⅓ cup), sifted
cream liqueur, such as Baileys	2 tablespoons
toasted flaked almonds	to serve

Lay a sheet of baking paper on a flat heatproof surface. Put the caster sugar and 1 teaspoon of cold water in a heavy-based frying pan. Heat over medium heat until the sugar begins to melt and change colour. Do not stir, but slowly turn the pan to swirl the contents together. When all the sugar has melted and turned golden, after about 6–8 minutes, remove the pan from the heat, add the almonds and swirl the pan to coat. Immediately pour the mixture onto the baking paper in a thin layer and leave to set for 20 minutes. Roughly break up the toffee with your hands, then chop it in a food processor until medium–fine.

Pour 200 ml (7 fl oz) of the cream into a small saucepan and heat for 3–4 minutes, or until hot but not boiling. Whisk the egg yolks and half the icing sugar in a large bowl until pale. Whisk in the cocoa powder. Add the hot cream and whisk until smooth.

Whip the remaining cream until soft peaks form. In a separate clean bowl, whisk the egg whites until soft peaks form, then gradually add the remaining icing sugar and continue whisking until thick and glossy. Using a metal spoon, gently fold the cream into the chocolate custard, then fold in the egg white mixture. Sprinkle half the crushed almond toffee onto the chocolate mixture and fold through, then repeat with the remaining almond toffee. Fold in the liqueur.

Line 6 x 250 ml (9 fl oz/1 cup) metal moulds with two thin strips of foil to use as handles when unmoulding the semifreddo. Divide the chocolate mixture among the moulds. Cover the tops with foil and freeze for at least 24 hours.

To serve, transfer the moulds to the refrigerator for 5 minutes, then use the foil handles to unmould the semifreddo. Top each with flaked almonds and serve immediately.

Don't stir the caramel; swirl the pan instead.

Work quickly as the nuts and caramel will set immediately.

lemon, fig and walnut cake with honey yoghurt .... serves 8–10

THIS DELIGHTFUL CAKE FEATURES ALMOST ALL OF THE CLASSIC ELEMENTS OF MEDITERRANEAN FOOD: FIGS, WALNUTS, LEMON, WHEAT AND OLIVE OIL. THE ONLY ELEMENT MISSING, OF COURSE, IS THE VINE, WHICH CAN BE EASILY INTRODUCED WITH A LITTLE GLASS OF SOMETHING APPROPRIATE.

caster (superfine) sugar	115 g (4 oz/½ cup)
fine semolina	310 g (11 oz/2½ cups)
ground almonds	150 g (5½ oz/1½ cups)
baking powder	3 teaspoons
bicarbonate of soda (baking soda)	½ teaspoon
lemon	1, zested and juiced
olive oil	125 ml (4 fl oz/½ cup)
eggs	2, at room temperature, beaten
Greek-style yoghurt	185 g (6½ oz/¾ cup)
milk	125 ml (4 fl oz/½ cup)
chopped walnuts	60 g (2¼ oz/½ cup)
fresh or semi-dried figs	7, chopped, plus 4 sliced

honey yoghurt

Greek-style yoghurt	250 g (9 oz/1 cup)
honey	90 g (3¼ oz/¼ cup)
natural vanilla extract	2 teaspoons

Preheat the oven to 180°C (350°F/Gas 4) and grease and line a 23 cm (9 inch) square cake tin.

Combine the sugar, semolina, ground almonds, baking powder and bicarbonate of soda in a large bowl. In a separate bowl, combine the lemon zest, lemon juice, olive oil, eggs, yoghurt and milk, then stir the lemon mixture into the semolina mixture. Fold in the walnuts and chopped figs. Pour the mixture into the tin, smooth the top and decorate with the extra sliced figs. Bake for 40 minutes, or until a skewer comes out clean when inserted into the cake.

Meanwhile, to make the honey yoghurt, put the yoghurt, honey and vanilla in a small bowl and stir to combine. Keep refrigerated until needed.

Serve the warm cake accompanied by the honey yoghurt.

A venerable old nut, the walnut has been cultivated since ancient Greek times. There are numerous varieties but the most common is the nut first grown by the ancient Persians: the Persian (English) walnut. When young, green walnuts can be eaten whole (but beware of their sour taste) or pickled. The mature nut has a hard shell, and the nut within is separated into two halves by an inedible papery membrane. Walnuts are used in sweet and savoury dishes; ground into flour; or pressed to release their oil. Store walnuts in their shells for up to three months in a cool, dry place, and shelled nuts in the refrigerator for up to six months.

profiteroles with coffee mascarpone and dark chocolate sauce..makes 16

CHOUX PASTRY DEPENDS FOR ITS SUCCESS ON STICKING CLOSELY TO THE RECIPE, BUT IT IS NOT NECESSARILY DIFFICULT TO MAKE. CHOUX IS CRISP AND WONDERFULLY LIGHT, AND PERFECT FOR FILLING WITH INDULGENT FLAVOURS. THE PROFITEROLES SHOULD BE EATEN FAIRLY SOON AFTER FILLING OR THE PASTRY WILL GO SOGGY.

plain (all-purpose) flour	125 g (4$\frac{1}{2}$ oz/1 cup)
unsalted butter	70 g (2$\frac{1}{2}$ oz), cubed
salt	$\frac{1}{2}$ teaspoon
eggs	4, at room temperature

filling

instant coffee granules	2 tablespoons
boiling water	1 tablespoon
mascarpone cheese	225 g (8 oz/1 cup)
icing (confectioners') sugar	2 tablespoons

dark chocolate sauce

good-quality dark chocolate	100 g (3$\frac{1}{2}$ oz/$\frac{2}{3}$ cup), chopped
unsalted butter	20 g ($\frac{3}{4}$ oz)
cream (whipping)	80 ml (2$\frac{1}{2}$ fl oz/$\frac{1}{3}$ cup)

Preheat the oven to 200°C (400°F/Gas 6) and lightly grease two baking trays.

Sift the flour onto a large piece of baking paper. Put the butter, salt and 250 ml (9 fl oz/1 cup) of water into a saucepan and bring to the boil, stirring occasionally. Using the baking paper as a funnel, pour the flour quickly into the boiling mixture. Reduce the heat to low, then beat vigorously with a wooden spoon until the mixture leaves the side of the pan and forms a smooth ball.

Transfer the mixture to a bowl and set aside to cool until it is lukewarm. Using electric beaters, beat in the eggs, one at a time, until the mixture is thick and glossy.

Using two spoons, gently drop 16 rounded balls of the mixture about 3 cm (1$\frac{1}{4}$ inches) in diameter and 3 cm (1$\frac{1}{4}$ inches) apart onto the prepared trays. Bake for 20 minutes, or until the balls are puffed. Reduce the oven to 180°C (350°F/Gas 4) and bake for another 10 minutes, or until the puffs are golden brown and crisp.

Using a small sharp knife, gently slit the puffs to allow the steam to escape, then return them to the oven for 10 minutes, or until the insides are dry. Set aside to cool to room temperature.

Meanwhile, to make the filling, dissolve the instant coffee in the boiling water. Set aside to cool. Beat the coffee, mascarpone and icing sugar until just combined. Be careful not to overmix or the mascarpone will split.

To make the dark chocolate sauce, put the chocolate, butter and cream in a small heatproof bowl over a small saucepan of simmering water, making sure the base of the bowl doesn't touch the water. Stir until combined. Set aside to cool slightly.

Just before serving, slit the profiteroles in half and sandwich together with the filling. Drizzle with the dark chocolate sauce, or serve the sauce separately.

vanilla custard log .... serves 6–8

IN THIS SIMPLE BUT SATISFYING DESSERT, CRISP FILO ENCASES A SILKY SMOOTH CUSTARD FLAVOURED WITH VANILLA AND ORANGE. DON'T BE FOOLED BY THE DELICATE APPEARANCE OF FILO — IT IS SURPRISINGLY HARDY. AS YOU WORK, KEEP THE SHEETS COVERED BY A CLEAN, DAMP CLOTH; THIS WILL ENSURE THEY REMAIN PLIABLE.

milk	750 ml (26 fl oz/3 cups)
cornflour (cornstarch)	50 g (1¾ oz/heaped ⅓ cup)
vanilla bean	1
egg yolks	6, at room temperature
caster (superfine) sugar	150 g (5½ oz/⅔ cup)
orange zest	2½ tablespoons finely grated
filo pastry	8 sheets
ghee or unsalted butter	40 g (1½ oz), melted
icing (confectioners') sugar	for dusting

Combine 60 ml (2 fl oz/¼ cup) of the milk with the cornflour and mix to a paste. Put the remaining milk in a saucepan over medium heat. Split the vanilla bean lengthways and scrape the seeds into the pan, discarding the pod. Add the cornflour paste, egg yolks, caster sugar and orange zest and whisk to combine. Boil, stirring, for 4 minutes, or until the custard is very thick. Remove from the heat, cover the surface with plastic wrap and set aside to cool.

Preheat the oven to 180°C (350°F/Gas 4). Line a baking tray with baking paper.

Brush a sheet of filo pastry with the melted ghee or butter. Top with a second sheet of filo, brush with ghee or butter, then repeat with two more sheets of pastry. Repeat with the remaining pastry so you have two rectangles of pastry. Spoon half the custard along the long edge of one rectangle of pastry, leaving a 9 cm (3½ inch) border, and shape into a 30 cm (12 inch) log. Carefully lift the border side of the pastry over the custard and roll up, tucking under the sides as you roll. Repeat with the remaining custard and pastry to make a second log.

Place the rolls on the prepared tray and brush with melted ghee or butter. Bake for 20 minutes, or until golden. Do not overcook the rolls or the custard will leak. Set aside to cool for 10 minutes. Dust with plenty of icing sugar before serving.

Stir the custard until it is very thick, then set aside to cool.

Make sure you leave a border around the custard.

Tuck in the sides as you roll up the logs.

pineapple gelato .... serves 4–6

IF USING FRESH PINEAPPLE, 1.5 KG (3 LB 5 OZ) WILL YIELD 250 ML (9 FL OZ/1 CUP) OF JUICE. CHOP AND PURÉE THE FLESH IN A FOOD PROCESSOR, THEN PUSH THROUGH A SIEVE. FOR ADDED RETRO APPEAL, SERVE THE SORBET IN THE PINEAPPLE SHELL, WITH OR WITHOUT PAPER UMBRELLAS.

caster (superfine) sugar	115 g (4 oz/½ cup)
fresh pineapple juice	250 ml (9 fl oz/1 cup)
lemon juice	60 ml (2 fl oz/¼ cup), strained
egg white	1, at room temperature

Combine the caster sugar with 250 ml (9 fl oz/1 cup) of water in a saucepan. Stir over low heat until the sugar has dissolved. Simmer for 10 minutes, then set aside to cool completely.

Add the pineapple juice and lemon juice to the sugar syrup and mix well. Pour the mixture into a 19 x 30 cm (7½ x 12 inch) cake tin and freeze for 1½ hours, or until the mixture is just frozen.

Once the mixture is just frozen, beat the egg white until stiff peaks form. Transfer the pineapple mixture to a bowl and beat with electric beaters until smooth. Fold the beaten egg white into the pineapple mixture, then return it to the tin. Cover with plastic wrap and freeze until set.

Alternatively, put the pineapple mixture in an ice-cream machine and churn following the manufacturer's instructions until just set. Fold in the beaten egg white, pour into the cake tin and freeze.

A native of tropical South America, the pineapple is actually several individual fruit joined together: each of these fruit are the result of numerous unfertilized flowers fused together. To most of us, however, it is a deliciously juicy and sweet fruit, the very emblem of warm weather. Like most fruit, pineapple is best eaten fresh, but it is also used in dishes such as ice creams, sorbets, cakes and as a controversial topping for pizza. Pineapples do not carry on ripening after being picked, so it pays to choose well. Select pineapples that are heavy for their size and sweetly aromatic.

hazelnut crackle log .... serves 6–8

EARLY FORMS OF MERINGUE WERE CALLED 'SUGAR PUFF', AND IT IS NOT HARD TO SEE WHY. CRISP AND CRACKLY, THE APPEAL OF MERINGUE COMES AS MUCH FROM ITS TEXTURE AS ITS TASTE. THIS MERINGUE ISN'T AS SWEET AS SOME, DUE TO THE HAZELNUTS, WHICH COMBINE WONDERFULLY WITH THE COFFEE MASCARPONE FILLING.

meringue

roasted skinned hazelnuts	70 g (2½ oz/½ cup)
egg whites	4, at room temperature
caster (superfine) sugar	150 g (5½ oz/⅔ cup)
cornflour (cornstarch)	1 teaspoon
natural vanilla extract	1 teaspoon
white wine vinegar	1 teaspoon

filling

instant coffee granules	2 teaspoons
hot water	2 teaspoons
mascarpone cheese	225 g (8 oz/1 cup)
icing (confectioners') sugar	2 tablespoons, sifted

To make the meringue, preheat the oven to 150°C (300°F/Gas 2). Draw a 20 x 35 cm (8 x 14 inch) rectangle on a sheet of baking paper. Put the sheet, pencil side down, on a baking tray.

Put the hazelnuts in a food processor and process until the nuts are coarsely ground.

Whisk the egg whites in a large bowl until soft peaks form. Gradually add the sugar, 1 tablespoon at a time, and whisk until stiff and glossy. Gently fold in the hazelnuts, then the cornflour, vanilla and vinegar. Spoon onto the baking tray and spread evenly inside the marked rectangle. Bake for 25 minutes, or until the meringue is set and lightly golden.

Lay a large sheet of baking paper on a work surface and invert the cooked meringue on top. Peel off the baking paper and set aside to cool for 15 minutes.

To make the filling, dissolve the instant coffee in the hot water. Put the coffee, mascarpone and icing sugar in a bowl and mix well.

Spread the filling evenly over the meringue. Starting at one short end and using the baking paper as a lever, gently roll up the meringue. The outer surface will crack into a pattern. Serve immediately, cut into slices.

Fold the hazelnuts into the egg white mixture.

Spread the mixture evenly using a palette knife.

Spread the filling to cover the whole meringue.

summer

This is the season when nature is at its most abundant, when exotic fruits such as delicately perfumed lychees, tart-yet-sweet passionfruit and red papaya become wonderfully, if fleetingly, available. Berries of all colours, shapes and sizes abound, as do stone fruits, from soft, furry peaches and apricots to firmer nectarines and cherries. Strong flavours, vibrant colours and heady aromas proclaim the arrival of summer.

Not surprisingly, there is a fair dose of the tropical in this chapter, with desserts such as coconut pavlovas topped with tropical fruits and passionfruit cream, and mango ice cream log doing their best to suggest languid days by the pool. Even dishes hailing from countries not renowned for their long, hot summer days get in on the act — the traditional English dessert Eton mess goes tropical with the addition of red papaya and passionfruit. The wonderful thing about cooking with fruit is its versatility: it can make the familiar special, for example by using caramelized peaches and passionfruit in a crumble tart; it can provide colour and at least the suggestion of healthiness to an otherwise frighteningly decadent recipe, such as the white chocolate roulade filled with vanilla cream and fresh berries, and it can also form wonderful desserts in its own right, like poached vanilla peaches with raspberry purée and passionfruit sauce.

However, it is perhaps in the realm of ice cream and sorbet that fruit comes into its own. This chapter includes a number of superb recipes, featuring peaches, mangoes, lychees and strawberries, combined with aromatic spices such as vanilla and star anise and fragrant waters such as rosewater. The results look wonderful and taste divine. An ice-cream machine is handy for these desserts, but not essential, and sorbet can be made with just a food processor.

Finally, though summer generally isn't the time when you want to be labouring in the kitchen, a few involved recipes have been included because they were too good to leave out — not everything need take only ten minutes! Individual cheesecakes with macerated strawberries are irresistibly good, the sweet, soft fruit contrasting perfectly with the rich, smooth cheesecake. Also, instructions are given for making perfect crepes — make a batch of these, fill them with fresh fruit and your own home-made ice cream and you are well on your way to a sensational summer.

individual cheesecakes with macerated strawberries..makes 12

SERVE THESE LITTLE CHEESECAKES AT THE END OF A MEAL AND YOU SHALL MAKE YOURSELF VERY POPULAR. RICH AND VELVETY, THEY ARE NOT BAKED BUT REFRIGERATED OVERNIGHT. THE ADVANTAGE OF THAT, OF COURSE, IS THAT ALL THE HARD WORK IS DONE WELL IN ADVANCE OF THE BIG OCCASION.

sweet biscuit (cookie) crumbs	100 g (3½ oz/heaped ¾ cup)
toasted flaked almonds	90 g (3¼ oz/1 cup), lightly crushed
white chocolate	90 g (3¼ oz/scant ⅔ cup) chopped, melted
unsalted butter	60 g (2¼ oz), melted

filling

powdered gelatine	2 teaspoons
cream cheese	250 g (9 oz/1 cup), softened
caster (superfine) sugar	90 g (3¼ oz/heaped ⅓ cup)
orange zest	1 teaspoon finely grated
orange juice	2 tablespoons
cream (whipping)	125 ml (4 fl oz/½ cup)
egg white	1, at room temperature

macerated strawberries

strawberries	500 g (1 lb 2 oz/3⅓ cups)
caster (superfine) sugar	1 tablespoon
orange zest	¼ teaspoon finely grated
orange juice	2 tablespoons

Lightly grease a 12-hole standard muffin tin. Line each hole with two long strips of baking paper in the shape of a cross to help remove the cheesecakes.

Put the biscuit crumbs, almonds, white chocolate and butter in a bowl and stir until just combined, adding more butter if the mixture is too dry. Divide the mixture among the muffin holes and use your fingers to press it over the bases and up the sides, smoothing with the back of a spoon. Refrigerate the crusts while preparing the filling.

To make the filling, put 1 tablespoon of water in a small bowl and sprinkle with the gelatine. Leave the gelatine to sponge and swell.

Beat the cream cheese, sugar and orange zest in a small bowl with electric beaters until light and creamy. Beat in the orange juice until combined. Stir in the gelatine mixture.

Whip the cream until soft peaks form. In a separate bowl, whisk the egg white with a clean whisk until soft peaks form. Fold the cream and egg white into the cream cheese mixture. Spoon into the prepared crusts and refrigerate for several hours or overnight, or until set.

To make the macerated strawberries, cut the strawberries into small pieces. Combine the strawberries with the sugar, orange zest and orange juice and refrigerate for several hours.

To serve, carefully remove the cheesecakes from the muffin tin and top with a spoonful of strawberries.

Smooth the biscuit crust with the back of a spoon.

Leave the strawberries for several hours to soak up the sauce.

tropical eton mess .... serves 4

THIS DESSERT MAKES NO PRETENCE OF SOPHISTICATION, WHICH MEANS IT WILL BE A SURE-FIRE WINNER WITH EVERYONE. THE FRUIT CAN BE CHANGED TO MATCH THE SEASON, THOUGH STICK WITH FRUIT THAT ARE JUICY BUT FIRM — YOU DON'T WANT A MUSHY MESS. IF YOU CHANGE THE FRUIT, SELECT COMPLEMENTARY LIQUEURS.

meringues

egg white	1, at room temperature
caster (superfine) sugar	55 g (2 oz/$1/4$ cup)
cornflour (cornstarch)	$1/4$ teaspoon
strawberries	125 g ($4^1/2$ oz/heaped $3/4$ cup), thickly sliced
small red papaya	$1/2$, seeded, peeled and cubed
passionfruit	4
caster (superfine) sugar	1 tablespoon
raspberry liqueur, such as Framboise, or orange liqueur, such as Grand Marnier	1 tablespoon, optional
thickened (whipping) cream	170 ml ($5^1/2$ fl oz/$2/3$ cup)
Greek-style yoghurt	175 g (6 oz/scant $3/4$ cup)

To make the meringues, preheat the oven to 130°C (250°F/Gas 1) and line a baking tray with baking paper.

Beat the egg white until stiff peaks form. Add 1 tablespoon of the caster sugar and beat for 3 minutes, or until glossy. Add another tablespoon of sugar and beat for another 3 minutes. Add the remaining sugar and the cornflour and beat for 2 minutes.

Put four even-sized heaped spoonfuls of the meringue mixture on the prepared tray. Bake for 30 minutes, or until the meringues are firm on the outside. Turn off the oven and leave them in the oven until the oven is cold. Roughly crumble the meringues.

Combine the strawberries, papaya and half the passionfruit pulp in a bowl. Stir in the sugar and the liqueur, if using. Set aside for 5 minutes, or until ready to assemble.

Just before serving, beat the cream in a bowl until thick. Stir in the yoghurt. Add the fruit mixture all at once and stir until roughly combined. Spoon half the mixture into 4 x 310 ml ($10^3/4$ fl oz/ $1^1/4$ cup) tall parfait glasses. Top with the crumbled meringue and then the remaining fruit. Garnish with the remaining passionfruit pulp and serve immediately.

Use two spoons to help put the meringue mixture on the tray.

Combine the fruit with the sugar and liqueur.

Mix the cream, yoghurt and fruit together briefly.

cherry clafoutis .... serves 8

FEW FRUIT ARRIVE WITH THE SORT OF UNBRIDLED COLOUR AND ABUNDANCE SHOWN BY CHERRIES EACH SUMMER. UNDOUBTEDLY, SUMMER IS THE BEST TIME TO MAKE THIS RECIPE. OUT OF SEASON, YOU CAN USE 680 G (1 LB 8 OZ/ 3½ CUPS) OF WELL-DRAINED, TINNED PITTED CHERRIES; MORELLO SOUR CHERRIES WILL GIVE THE BEST RESULT.

cherries	500 g (1 lb 2 oz) unpitted, stems removed
plain (all-purpose) flour	60 g (2¼ oz/½ cup)
caster (superfine) sugar	90 g (3¼ oz/heaped ⅓ cup)
eggs	2, at room temperature, lightly beaten
milk	200 ml (7 fl oz)
natural vanilla extract	1 teaspoon
unsalted butter	20 g (¾ oz), melted
icing (confectioners') sugar	for dusting

Preheat the oven to 210°C (415°F/Gas 6–7) and lightly grease a 1.5 litre (52 fl oz/6 cup) capacity round ovenproof dish.

Spread the cherries evenly over the base of the prepared dish.

Put the flour, caster sugar and a pinch of salt in a bowl and stir to combine. Add the eggs and beat until well combined. Combine the milk, vanilla and butter, then pour into the egg mixture and beat until combined.

Carefully pour the batter over the cherries and bake for 40 minutes, or until the clafoutis is golden brown. Set aside to cool for at least 10 minutes, then serve warm or cold, dusted with icing sugar.

The glossy, deep-red cherry has been celebrated throughout the centuries by artists and poets, gardeners and cooks alike. A relative of the plum, peach and apricot, today there are many hundreds of varieties, which are classified as either sweet, sour or hybrid. Sweet cherries and hybrids can be eaten raw or cooked, while sour cherries are mostly reserved for cooking, for example, in pies and jams. When buying cherries, look at the stems: they should be soft and pliable, not brown and brittle. Sweet cherries can be stored in the refrigerator for up to one week, and sour cherries for several weeks. Cherries are also used to make Kirsch and maraschino liqueur.

blueberry crumble cake .... serves 8–10

THIS CAKE IS QUICK AND EASY TO MAKE AND, APART FROM A FEW FRESH INGREDIENTS, RELIES ON STORE-CUPBOARD STAPLES. IT HAS A SATISFYING, FIRM TEXTURE AND CRUMBLY, SWEET TOPPING. BLUEBERRIES ARE MOST OFTEN PAIRED WITH ALMONDS, BUT HERE PECANS ARE USED TO EQUALLY GOOD EFFECT.

plain (all-purpose) flour	125 g (4½ oz/1 cup)
wholemeal (whole-wheat) plain (all-purpose) flour	110 g (3¾ oz/¾ cup)
caster (superfine) sugar	225 g (8 oz/1 cup)
baking powder	2½ teaspoons
ground cinnamon	½ teaspoon
blueberries	150 g (5½ oz/1 cup)
egg	1, at room temperature
milk	185 ml (6 fl oz/¾ cup)
oil	80 ml (2½ fl oz/⅓ cup)
natural vanilla extract	1 teaspoon
lemon	1, zest finely grated
thick (double/heavy) cream	to serve

topping

pecans	60 g (2¼ oz/½ cup) chopped
soft brown sugar	55 g (2 oz/⅓ cup)
plain (all-purpose) flour	30 g (1 oz/¼ cup)
blueberries	150 g (5½ oz/1 cup)
oil	2 tablespoons

Preheat the oven to 190°C (375°F/Gas 5) and grease a 20 cm (8 inch) spring-form cake tin.

Sift the flours, sugar, baking powder and cinnamon into a large bowl. Return the husks collected in the sieve to the bowl. Toss the blueberries through the flour mixture.

Whisk together the egg, milk, oil, vanilla and lemon zest. Pour into the dry ingredients and stir to combine. Pour the mixture into the prepared tin.

To make the topping, combine the pecans, brown sugar, flour and blueberries in a bowl and sprinkle evenly over the cake. Drizzle the oil over the topping.

Bake the cake for 50–55 minutes, or until a skewer comes out clean when inserted into the cake. Serve the cake warm with a dollop of thick cream.

Toss the blueberries through the dry ingredients.

Combine the egg mixture with the dry ingredients.

Sprinkle the topping evenly over the cake.

mango ice cream log .... serves 8–10

UNLIKE MANY ICE CREAMS, WHICH ARE SERVED AS AN ACCOMPANIMENT, THIS ICE CREAM LOG DESERVES TO TAKE CENTRE STAGE. THE GOLDEN FRUITY FRESHNESS OF THE MANGO PROVIDES A CONTRAST TO THE CREAMY LAYERS SURROUNDING IT. SERVE THE ICE CREAM WITH ALMOND BISCOTTI OR OTHER THIN CRISP BISCUITS.

cream (whipping)	500 ml (17 fl oz/2 cups)
milk	250 ml (9 fl oz/1 cup)
vanilla bean	1, split lengthways
egg yolks	6, at room temperature
caster (superfine) sugar	115 g (4 oz/1/2 cup)
mangoes	2 large, flesh puréed

Put the cream and milk in a saucepan. Scrape the seeds from the vanilla bean into the saucepan and add the vanilla pod. Heat over medium heat until the mixture is hot but not boiling. Remove from the heat and discard the vanilla pod.

Using electric beaters, beat the egg yolks and caster sugar in a large bowl until thick and pale. Slowly pour the hot cream mixture onto the egg mixture, whisking continuously. Pour the custard into a clean saucepan and stir over low heat for 5–6 minutes, or until the custard is thick enough to coat the back of a spoon. Refrigerate until completely cold.

Pour the custard into an ice-cream machine and churn according to the manufacturer's instructions. Alternatively, pour the custard into a metal bowl and freeze for 2–2 1/2 hours, or until set around the edges but still soft in the middle; beat with electric beaters for 3 minutes, or until the custard is smooth again. Once the mixture is churned or smooth, pour half the mixture into an 8 x 19 cm (3 1/4 x 7 1/2 inch) loaf (bar) tin lined with plastic wrap. Refrigerate the remaining mixture until required. Carefully spoon the mango purée over the mixture in the tin and freeze for 1 hour. Top with the remaining ice cream mixture and freeze overnight.

To serve, dip the base of the tin in hot water for 5 seconds, then invert the ice cream onto a serving plate and cut into slices.

The easiest way to access the flesh is to cut into the cheeks.

Carefully spoon the mango purée over the first layer of ice cream.

Add the top layer of ice cream after freezing the log for 1 hour.

poached vanilla peaches with raspberry purée and passionfruit sauce .... serves 4

THIS DELIGHTFUL DESSERT IS EXACTLY WHAT SUMMER ENTERTAINING SHOULD BE ALL ABOUT: A SIMPLE, QUICK RECIPE, FULL OF FLAVOUR AND COLOUR, THAT UTILIZES THE BEST OF THE SEASON'S PRODUCE. YOU WILL NEED ABOUT THREE PASSIONFRUIT FOR THIS RECIPE.

caster (superfine) sugar	350 g (12 oz/1½ cups)
vanilla bean	1, halved lengthways
peaches	4
fresh raspberries or frozen raspberries, thawed	100 g (3½ oz/heaped ¾ cup)
vanilla ice cream	4 small scoops

passionfruit sauce

passionfruit pulp	60 ml (2 fl oz/¼ cup)
caster (superfine) sugar	2 tablespoons

Put the sugar, vanilla bean and 625 ml (21½ fl oz/2½ cups) of water in a large saucepan. Stir over low heat until the sugar has dissolved. Bring to a slow boil, then add the peaches and simmer for 5 minutes, or until the peaches are just tender and softened. Cool the peaches in the syrup, then remove with a slotted spoon. Peel and halve the peaches, removing the stones.

Put the raspberries in a food processor and process until puréed. Push the raspberries through a sieve, discarding the pulp.

To make the passionfruit sauce, combine the passionfruit pulp with the sugar and stir until the sugar has dissolved.

To serve, divide the raspberry purée among 4 glasses. Arrange a scoop of ice cream and two peach halves on top. Spoon over the passionfruit sauce and serve immediately.

This fragrant, juicy stone fruit is instantly recognizable by its rosy pink, downy skin. Inside, the flesh of the peach may be yellow or white, separating easily from the stone (freestone) or not (clingstone). Peaches do not last long, so buy only as many as can be eaten or cooked within the space of three to four days. Avoid bruised or soft peaches; the latter will taste floury and be sadly disappointing. Apart from enjoying their succulent flesh just as it is, peaches are excellent for poaching in wine or syrup and for using in tarts, sorbets and sauces.

apricot meringue torte .... serves 8–10

APRICOTS COMBINE WELL WITH BOTH SAVOURY AND SWEET FLAVOURS, BUT THEIR SHORT SEASON MEANS THEY DON'T OFTEN MAKE IT INTO THE KITCHEN ── A GREAT PITY, AS THIS DESSERT SHOWS. IF USING FRESH APRICOTS, MAKE SURE THEY ARE SWEET, FIRM AND RIPE; OTHERWISE USE TINNED APRICOTS.

caster (superfine) sugar	375 g (13 oz/1²/³ cups)
cinnamon stick	1
natural vanilla extract	2 teaspoons
apricots	450 g (1 lb), quartered, stones removed
egg whites	6, at room temperature
white vinegar	1¹/² teaspoons
ground hazelnuts	35 g (1¹/⁴ oz/¹/³ cup)
thickened (whipping) cream	300 ml (10¹/² fl oz)
icing (confectioners') sugar	for dusting

Combine 375 ml (13 fl oz/1¹/² cups) of water, 125 g (4¹/² oz/ heaped ¹/² cup) of the sugar, the cinnamon stick and 1 teaspoon of the vanilla in a large saucepan. Stir over low heat until the sugar has dissolved. Increase the heat to medium and simmer for 15 minutes. Add the quartered apricots and simmer over low heat for another 40 minutes, or until the apricots are thick and pulpy. Set aside to cool.

Preheat the oven to 150°C (300°F/Gas 2) and draw a 22 cm (8¹/² inch) circle on two sheets of baking paper. Put the sheets, pencil side down, on two baking trays.

Beat the egg whites in a bowl until stiff peaks form. Add the remaining sugar, a little at a time, and continue beating until the mixture is stiff and glossy. Beat in the vinegar and remaining vanilla. Gently fold in the ground hazelnuts.

Divide the meringue mixture between the two circles on the prepared trays and smooth the surface. Bake for 35–40 minutes, or until the meringues are firm and dry. Turn off the oven and leave the meringues in the oven to cool completely.

Peel off the baking paper and place one meringue disc on a serving plate. Whip the cream until stiff peaks form. Discard the cinnamon stick from the syrup and drain the apricots. Gently stir the apricots through the whipped cream and spread over the meringue. Place the second meringue disc on top of the apricot cream and dust with icing sugar.

Simmer the apricots until thick and pulpy.

Gently stir the apricot mixture into the cream.

mango and star anise sorbet with honey macadamia wafers

. . . . serves 6

USE THE HONEY MACADAMIA WAFERS AS SPOONS FOR SCOOPING UP THIS SUMMER SORBET: SMOOTH, GENTLY PERFUMED SORBET AGAINST SWEET, NUTTY CRUNCHINESS. PERFECT. STAR ANISE WILL BRING A SUBTLE ANISEED FLAVOUR TO THE SORBET.

caster (superfine) sugar	185 g (6½ oz/heaped ¾ cup)
star anise	2
lemon juice	1 tablespoon
mangoes	3, flesh chopped to give 500 g (1 lb 2 oz)
egg white	1, at room temperature

honey macadamia wafers

egg white	1, at room temperature
caster (superfine) sugar	60 g (2¼ oz/¼ cup)
honey	2 tablespoons
plain (all-purpose) flour	2 tablespoons, sifted
unsalted butter	40 g (1½ oz), melted and cooled
macadamia nuts	100 g (3½ oz/¾ cup) chopped

Combine the sugar with 310 ml (10¾ fl oz/1¼ cups) of water and the star anise in a saucepan. Stir over medium heat until the sugar has dissolved. Bring to the boil, then reduce the heat and simmer for 1 minute. Set aside to cool to room temperature. Stir in the lemon juice.

Put the mango in a food processor and purée until smooth. Strain the sugar syrup onto the mango and process until just combined, then transfer to a shallow metal container, cover and freeze. When the sorbet is three-quarters frozen, transfer it to a food processor, add the egg white and blend until smooth. Return the sorbet to the container and freeze until required.

To make the honey macadamia wafers, preheat the oven to 200°C (400°F/Gas 6). Line two 30 cm (12 inch) square baking trays with baking paper. Put the egg white in a small bowl and beat with electric beaters until soft peaks form. Gradually add the sugar and continue beating until the sugar has dissolved. Beat in the honey and then fold in the flour and butter. Spread the mixture very thinly over the prepared trays, then sprinkle evenly with the macadamia nuts. Bake for 7–10 minutes, or until lightly golden. Set aside to cool on the trays, then break into pieces. Store in an airtight container as the wafers will soften on standing. Serve scoops of mango sorbet accompanied by large pieces of the honey macadamia wafers.

Strain the star anise syrup onto the mango purée.

Sprinkle the macadamia nuts in an even layer.

three ways with raspberries

BURSTING WITH COLOUR AND FLAVOUR, RASPBERRIES ARE NOT REALLY TEAM PLAYERS, NOT WHERE OTHER FRUIT ARE CONCERNED AT ANY RATE. INSTEAD, THEY PREFER THE COMPANY OF INGREDIENTS SUCH AS CREAM, CHOCOLATE AND CHAMPAGNE. FRESH RASPBERRIES ARE DELICATE AND SHOULD BE HANDLED AS LITTLE AS POSSIBLE. THEY DO FREEZE WELL, HOWEVER, SO IF YOU ARE IN NEED OF A LITTLE CHEER IN WINTER, MAKE THE RICE PUDDING WITH FROZEN RASPBERRIES — A BOLD DASH OF RASPBERRY CUTTING THROUGH WHITE CHOCOLATE CREAMINESS.

raspberry and orange trifle

Combine 500 ml (17 fl oz/2 cups) good-quality ready-made custard, 250 g (9 oz/1 heaped cup) mascarpone cheese, 120 g (4¼ oz/ ½ cup) puréed raspberries, 40 g (1½ oz/⅓ cup) icing (confectioners') sugar and 60 g (2¼ oz/1¼ cups) lightly crushed ready-made meringues. Arrange 250 g (9 oz) sliced plain orange cake or 4 sliced orange muffins in the base of a large glass dish or 6 dessert glasses. Sprinkle 60 ml (2 fl oz/¼ cup) orange liqueur, such as Cointreau, over the cake, then sprinkle with 250 g (9 oz/2 cups) raspberries. Spoon the custard mixture over the raspberries and top with another 125 g (4½ oz/1 cup) raspberries and 40 g (1½ oz/ 1¼ cups) crushed meringues. Chill until ready to serve. Dust with sifted icing (confectioners') sugar, if desired. Serves 6.

raspberry, lemon grass and sparkling rosé jellies

Put 400 g (14 oz/3¼ cups) raspberries, 225 g (8 oz/1 cup) caster (superfine) sugar, 2 bruised lemon grass stems, 60 ml (2 fl oz/ ¼ cup) lemon juice and 375 ml (13 fl oz/1½ cups) sparkling rosé in a saucepan. Slowly bring to the boil. Boil for 1 minute, then set aside for 30 minutes. Strain the mixture through muslin into a bowl, discarding the pulp. Return the liquid to a clean saucepan and heat to just below boiling point. Whisk in 4½ teaspoons powdered gelatine until dissolved, or soften two 4 g (⅓ oz) gelatine sheets in water, squeeze out the excess water and stir into the raspberry liquid until the gelatine has dissolved. Set aside to cool. Stir another 375 ml (13 fl oz/1½ cups) sparkling rosé into the raspberry liquid. Divide 100 g (3½ oz/heaped ¾ cup) raspberries among 6 champagne flutes. Pour a little of the raspberry syrup into each glass to set the raspberries, then refrigerate. Refrigerate the remaining jelly until it is cold and near setting point. Whisk the cold jelly to create bubbles, then pour it into the glasses and chill until set. Serves 6.

white chocolate and raspberry ripple rice pudding

Using a hand blender, purée 120 g (4¼ oz/1 cup) fresh raspberries, 2 tablespoons icing (confectioners') sugar and 2 tablespoons raspberry liqueur, such as Framboise. Melt 30 g (1 oz) unsalted butter in a large non-stick saucepan. Add 125 g (4½ oz/heaped ½ cup) risotto rice and 1 split vanilla bean and stir until the rice is coated in the butter. Heat 800 ml (28 fl oz) milk, 50 g (1¾ oz/¼ cup) caster (superfine) sugar and 1 teaspoon natural vanilla extract to just below boiling point. Ladle a spoonful of the milk mixture into the rice and stir constantly until the liquid has been absorbed. Repeat the process until all the milk mixture has been added. Remove the vanilla bean. Add 100 g (3½ oz/⅔ cup) chopped white chocolate and stir until the chocolate has melted. Set aside for 5 minutes, then spoon the rice pudding into bowls. Swirl the raspberry purée through the rice to create a ripple effect. Serves 4.

lychee and strawberry ice cream................serves 6–8

ANYONE WHO HAS NEVER TRIED LYCHEES BEFORE WILL WONDER WHAT GIVES THIS ICE CREAM SUCH A WONDERFUL PERFUMED SWEETNESS — SOMETHING BESIDES THE STRAWBERRIES. THESE TWO FRUIT COMBINE VERY WELL, DESPITE THE FACT THAT ONE IS FROM TEMPERATE REGIONS AND THE OTHER NATIVE TO TROPICAL CHINA.

strawberries	250 g (9 oz/1²/₃ cups)
caster (superfine) sugar	165 g (5³/₄ oz/³/₄ cup)
lychees in syrup	565 g (1 lb 4 oz) tin
milk	375 ml (13 fl oz/1¹/₂ cups)
cream (whipping)	500 ml (17 fl oz/2 cups)
egg yolks	6, at room temperature

Reserve 50 g (1³/₄ oz/¹/₃ cup) of the strawberries for decoration. Hull and roughly chop the remaining strawberries and place in a bowl, along with any juices. Sprinkle with 1 tablespoon of the sugar and set aside for 30 minutes. Drain and finely chop the lychees, reserving 125 ml (4 fl oz/¹/₂ cup) of the syrup.

Put the milk, cream and remaining sugar in a saucepan over medium heat. Cook, stirring constantly, for a few minutes, or until the sugar has dissolved and the milk is just about to boil. Remove from the heat.

Whisk the egg yolks in a bowl for 1 minute, or until combined, then add 60 ml (2 fl oz/¹/₄ cup) of the hot milk mixture. Stir to combine, then pour into the remaining milk mixture. Return the saucepan to low–medium heat and cook, stirring constantly with a wooden spoon, until the mixture thickens and coats the back of the spoon. Do not allow the mixture to boil. Strain through a fine sieve and set aside to cool.

Gently stir the strawberries and any juice, lychees and lychee syrup into the custard to combine. Transfer to an ice-cream machine and freeze according to the manufacturer's instructions. Alternatively, transfer to a shallow metal tray and freeze, whisking every couple of hours until the ice cream is frozen and creamy in texture. Serve the ice cream with the reserved strawberries.

Leave the chopped strawberries to soak up the sugar.

Strain the custard to give a silky-smooth ice cream.

nectarine feuilletées .... makes 8

WHEN NECTARINES ARE IN FULL FLIGHT IN SUMMER, IT'S NICE TO BE ABLE TO GRAB A HANDFUL AND MAKE A
FABULOUS DESSERT WITHOUT HAVING TO THINK ABOUT IT TOO MUCH. THIS IS JUST SUCH A DESSERT. THE NAME
OF THIS RECIPE COMES FROM THE FRENCH 'PÂTÉ FEUILLETÉE', MEANING PUFF PASTRY.

frozen butter puff pastry	2 sheets, thawed
unsalted butter	50 g (1³/4 oz), softened
ground almonds	55 g (2 oz/¹/2 cup)
natural vanilla extract	¹/2 teaspoon
nectarines	5 large
caster (superfine) sugar	55 g (2 oz/¹/4 cup)
apricot or peach jam	110 g (3³/4 oz/¹/3 cup), warmed and sieved

Preheat the oven to 200°C (400°F/Gas 6). Line two large baking trays with baking paper.

Cut the pastry sheets into 8 x 12 cm (4¹/2 inch) rounds and place on the prepared trays. Combine the butter, ground almonds and vanilla in a small bowl to form a paste. Divide the paste among the pastry rounds and spread evenly, leaving a 1.5 cm (⁵/8 inch) border around the edge.

Halve the nectarines, removing the stones, and cut them into 5 mm (¹/4 inch) slices. Arrange the nectarine slices over the pastry rounds, overlapping the slices and leaving a thin border. Sprinkle the sugar over the nectarines.

Bake for 15 minutes, or until the pastries are puffed and golden. Brush the nectarines and pastry with the warm jam while the pastries are hot. Serve hot or at room temperature.

Smooth-skinned nectarines are sometimes passed over for their downy relative, the peach, but one is not better than the other; they are just different. Peaches are sweeter and more fragrant; nectarines are richer — their name stems from the Greek word for nectar. Like peaches, however, their flesh may be white or yellow, freestone or clingstone, with the white-fleshed fruit generally considered the most flavoursome. Nectarines are best bought fresh, not tinned. Select fruit that have good colour and smell, ripe but not to the point of being soft and squishy. Nectarines can be poached, stuffed and baked, grilled (broiled) and added to tarts and pastries.

aromatic peaches with sweetened greek yoghurt .... serves 4

THIS FRAGRANT, HEADY DESSERT INFUSES PEACHES WITH FOUR DIFFERENT SPICES — A DELECTABLE DISH TAKING FULL ADVANTAGE OF THE SEASON'S STONE FRUITS. MACERATE THE PEACHES IN THE SYRUP FOR NO LONGER THAN 4 HOURS OR THE PEACHES WILL DISCOLOUR AND LOSE THEIR BEAUTIFUL BLUSH.

caster (superfine) sugar	225 g (8 oz/1 cup)
vanilla bean	1, split lengthways
cinnamon stick	1
cardamom pods	6
star anise	2
peaches	4
dark brown sugar	2 tablespoons
Greek-style yoghurt	300 g (10½ oz/1¼ cups)

Pour 500 ml (17 fl oz/2 cups) of water into a saucepan and add the caster sugar. Heat over medium heat until the sugar has dissolved. Scrape the seeds from the vanilla bean into the saucepan and add the pod, cinnamon stick, cardamom pods and star anise. Boil for 2 minutes, then set aside to cool.

Put the peaches in a heatproof bowl and cover with boiling water. Set aside for 1 minute, then drain the peaches and refresh in ice-cold water. Halve the peaches, removing the stones and skin. Working quickly to prevent the peaches from browning, place the peaches in a bowl and strain the cooled syrup over them. Refrigerate for several hours to allow the peaches to macerate in the syrup.

Stir the dark brown sugar through the yoghurt and serve with the peaches and syrup.

Infuse the syrup with the aromatic spices.

Soak the peaches in boiling water to make them easy to peel.

Sweeten the yoghurt with a little dark brown sugar.

strawberry and
mascarpone mousse .... serves 6

FOR A TRIPLE-CREAM CHEESE, MASCARPONE IS NOT OVERLY SWEET. IT IS, HOWEVER, VERY RICH, MELLOW AND WONDERFULLY SMOOTH. IT PROVIDES THE PERFECT BASE FOR THE STRAWBERRIES AND CRUNCHY PRALINE. THIS RECIPE IS A GREAT ONE TO HAVE ON HAND FOR SUMMER, WHEN SWEET, JUICY STRAWBERRIES ARE AT THEIR PEAK.

caster (superfine) sugar	80 g (2¾ oz/⅓ cup)
powdered gelatine	1 tablespoon
strawberries	500 g (1 lb 2 oz/3⅓ cups), hulled
mascarpone cheese	250 g (9 oz/1 cup)
home-made crushed praline	to serve, optional (page 27)

Combine the sugar and 125 ml (4 fl oz/½ cup) of water in a small saucepan. Stir over low heat for 3 minutes, or until the sugar has dissolved. Sprinkle the gelatine over the sugar mixture and stir for 2 minutes, or until the gelatine has dissolved. Set aside to cool.

Put the hulled strawberries in a food processor and process until smooth. Add the mascarpone and process until well combined. With the motor running, add the gelatine mixture in a slow stream. Pour the mixture into a 1 litre (35 fl oz/4 cup) mould. Refrigerate overnight, or until set.

To serve, dip the base of the mould in hot water for 10 seconds, then invert the mousse onto a plate. Top with the crushed praline, if using.

This luscious fruit needs little introduction. Native to both Europe and America, the strawberry is grown in temperate regions around the world and is often available year-round. Look out for wild species, too, which can be more flavoursome than the cultivated varieties. The strawberry is unique in that the seeds grow around the outside of the fruit rather than inside it. Versatile and robust, strawberries can be used in everything from smoothies and purées to cakes and preserves. When buying, don't necessarily choose the biggest and brightest; rather, select those that are plump, glossy, unbruised and firm. Store in the refrigerator and only wash just before eating.

coconut pavlovas with tropical fruits and passionfruit cream... serves 4

WHO DOESN'T GET EXCITED BY A CRISP MERINGUE BASE, LADEN WITH CREAM AND FRESH FRUIT? THE PASSIONFRUIT CREAM USED HERE IS A CLASSIC TOPPING, THOUGH THE LYCHEES AND PAPAYA ARE A SIGN OF HOW THINGS CHANGE. HOWEVER, ANY SEASONAL FRESH FRUIT CAN BE USED.

pavlovas

egg whites	2, at room temperature
caster (superfine) sugar	115 g (4 oz/½ cup)
cornflour (cornstarch)	½ teaspoon
natural vanilla extract	½ teaspoon
shredded coconut	15 g (½ oz/¼ cup)

passionfruit cream

cream (whipping)	250 ml (9 fl oz/1 cup)
icing (confectioners') sugar	2 tablespoons
passionfruit	4
red papaya	½ small, seeded and peeled
fresh lychees	4, halved and seeded
mango	½, peeled and seeded

To make the pavlovas, preheat the oven to 120°C (235°F/Gas ½). Line a baking tray with baking paper.

Beat the egg whites and sugar in a bowl for 8 minutes, or until the meringue is glossy and very thick. Beat in the cornflour and vanilla, then gently fold the shredded coconut through the meringue mixture with a metal spoon.

Using two large metal tablespoons, spoon four large oval-shaped spoonfuls of meringue mixture onto the prepared tray. Bake for 30 minutes, or until the pavlovas are crisp on the outside. Turn off the oven and leave the pavlovas in the oven until the oven is cold.

To make the passionfruit cream, beat the cream and icing sugar until firm peaks form. Fold the passionfruit pulp through the cream and refrigerate until ready to serve.

Cut the papaya, lychees and mango into very small dice. To serve, top the pavlovas with some of the passionfruit cream and accompany with the diced fruit.

Note: For a quick alternative, make the meringues and top with whipped cream, a selection of fresh berries and a quick coulis made from puréed and sieved berries.

Use a metal spoon to fold in the shredded coconut.

Make sure the meringues are well spaced on the tray.

Gently fold the passionfruit pulp into the cream.

white chocolate and berry roulade . . . . serves 6–8

IT IS REMARKABLE HOW MANY SUPERB CREATIONS CAN BE MADE OUT OF THE BASIC ELEMENTS OF FLOUR, EGGS, SUGAR AND CREAM. ROULADES CAN BE SAVOURY, THOUGH THIS ONE MOST CERTAINLY ISN'T. BUY THE BEST JUICY BERRIES YOU CAN FIND TO REALLY BRING IT ALIVE.

eggs	4, at room temperature, separated
caster (superfine) sugar	115 g (4 oz/$\frac{1}{2}$ cup), plus extra, for sprinkling
hot water	1 tablespoon
white chocolate	60 g (2$\frac{1}{4}$ oz/heaped $\frac{1}{3}$ cup) finely grated
self-raising flour	60 g (2$\frac{1}{4}$ oz/$\frac{1}{2}$ cup)
strawberries	100 g (3$\frac{1}{2}$ oz/$\frac{2}{3}$ cup) sliced
fresh raspberries	100 g (3$\frac{1}{2}$ oz/heaped $\frac{3}{4}$ cup)
caster (superfine) sugar	1–2 tablespoons, to taste
thickened (whipping) cream	185 ml (6 fl oz/$\frac{3}{4}$ cup)
icing (confectioners') sugar	2 teaspoons, plus extra, for dusting
natural vanilla extract	1 teaspoon

Preheat the oven to 200°C (400°F/Gas 6). Lightly spray or grease a 25 x 30 cm (10 x 12 inch) Swiss roll tin (jelly roll tin) with oil. Line the tin with baking paper, allowing the paper to hang over the two long sides.

Beat the egg yolks and sugar with electric beaters for 5 minutes, or until very thick and creamy. Fold in the hot water and grated white chocolate. Sift the flour over the mixture and gently fold through until just combined.

Beat the egg whites with clean electric beaters until soft peaks form. Using a large metal spoon, fold the egg whites through the chocolate mixture until just combined. Pour the mixture into the prepared tin and bake for 12–15 minutes, or until the roulade is golden brown and firm to the touch.

Put a large sheet of baking paper on a flat surface and sprinkle with caster sugar. Turn the roulade out onto the sugared paper. Trim any crisp edges and roll up from the short end with the aid of the baking paper. Set aside for 5 minutes, then unroll and leave to cool.

Meanwhile, put the berries in a bowl and sweeten them with caster sugar, to taste. Beat the cream, icing sugar and vanilla until firm peaks form. Spread the roulade with the cream and sprinkle the berries over the top. Roll up and dust with icing sugar. Cut into slices to serve.

Use the baking paper to help roll up the roulade.

Sprinkle the berries evenly over the cream.

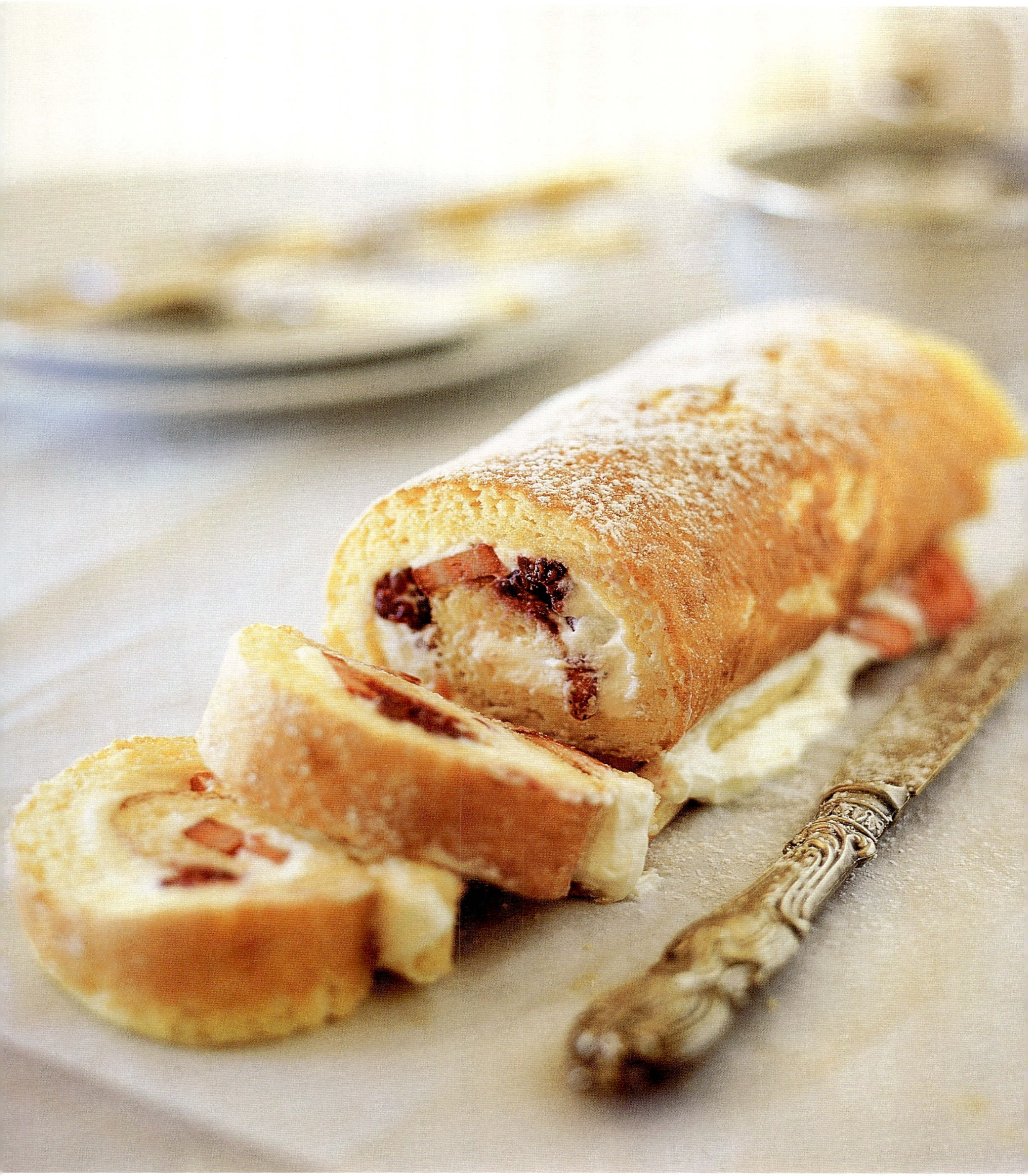

peach and rosewater sorbet .... serves 4–6

THE BEAUTY OF SORBETS IS THAT THEY ARE EASY TO MAKE: THEY REQUIRE FEW INGREDIENTS AND NO SPECIAL EQUIPMENT. ALL THAT IS NEEDED IS THE TIME TO FREEZE AND WHISK THE SORBET THOROUGHLY. THIS SWEETLY SCENTED AND FLAVOURED SORBET CAN BE DECORATED WITH UNSPRAYED ROSE PETALS.

peach tea	400 ml (14 fl oz)
caster (superfine) sugar	300 g (10½ oz/1⅓ cups)
peaches	6
rosewater	80 ml (2½ fl oz/⅓ cup)

Pour half the peach tea into a small saucepan. Add the sugar and stir until the sugar has dissolved. Bring to the boil and cook for 2 minutes, then remove from the heat and set aside to cool.

Quarter the peaches, removing the stones. Put the peaches and remaining peach tea in a saucepan and poach for 10 minutes. Remove the peaches with a slotted spoon, reserving the liquid, and peel off the skin. Set aside to cool.

Using a hand blender or small food processor, purée the peaches, poaching liquid, sugar syrup and rosewater until smooth. Pour the mixture into a plastic container and freeze for 1½ hours, or until the sides and base have frozen and the middle is a soft slush.

Using a food processor or hand blender, process until the mixture is evenly slushy. Repeat the freezing and processing at least twice, then freeze for another 30–60 minutes.

Rosewater is an expensive flower water that is made by distilling the fragrance of rose petals, most commonly the damask rose. The technique has been known since ancient Egyptian times but the use of rosewater reached its most lavish heights in the sumptuous cooking of Persia around the tenth century AD. Its popularity spread across the Middle East to India and Europe and it is still used to flavour traditional dishes such as Turkish delight, baklava and lassi, as well as to add a sweet fragrance to curries and rice dishes. Rosewater should be used only sparingly; otherwise dishes can take on a cloying sweetness.

the perfect crepe

Crepes are made using a sweetened batter of flour, milk, melted butter and eggs. At their simplest, they are eaten with a dusting of sugar and a squeeze of lemon, or they can be wrapped around a filling or soaked in a sauce. It's important to let the batter stand to allow the gluten in the flour to relax, thus allowing the maximum amount of liquid to be absorbed. Secondly, and perhaps most importantly, don't touch the crepe while the first side is cooking.

If making several crepes at once, stack them between sheets of baking paper, then either keep them warm in a low oven, or store them in the fridge. They freeze well when wrapped first in foil and then plastic wrap.

To make perfect crepes, sift 150 g (5½ oz/1¼ cups) plain (all-purpose) flour, a pinch of salt and 1 teaspoon sugar into a large bowl. Make a well in the centre. Whisk together 3 eggs and 435 ml (15¼ fl oz/1¾ cups) milk. Slowly pour into the well in the dry ingredients, whisking constantly and gradually drawing in the flour. Whisk in 80 g (2¾ oz) melted unsalted butter, then pour the batter into a container with a pouring lip. The batter should be the consistency of cream (whipping). Stand the batter in the refrigerator for 30 minutes.

Heat a crepe pan or non-stick frying pan over medium heat. Brush with a little melted unsalted butter, then pour in enough batter to form a thin layer, tilting and swirling the pan so the batter evenly covers the base. Tip out any excess batter and fill in any holes as necessary. Cook for about 1 minute without touching, or until the edge of the crepe starts to lift and the underside is golden brown. Use a palette knife to loosen the edge, and shake the pan to ensure the crepe isn't stuck. Carefully slide the palette knife under the crepe and flip it over. Cook for another 20–30 seconds, then slide the crepe onto a plate. Continue with the remaining batter, adding a little extra melted butter between crepes if necessary. Makes about 12.

caramelized peach and passionfruit crumble tart

USING READY-MADE SHORTCRUST (PIE) PASTRY MAKES THIS TART A WONDERFULLY QUICK RECIPE. CHOOSE A GOOD-QUALITY BUTTERY ONE AND LET IT SIT FOR 20 MINUTES BEFORE ROLLING OUT OR IT WILL CRACK AND BE DIFFICULT TO WORK WITH. THE CARAMELIZED PEACHES BRING A MELLOW RICHNESS TO THIS DESSERT.

ready-made shortcrust (pie) pastry	310 g (11 oz)
	or 1 quantity from page 134
plain (all-purpose) flour	80 g (2¾ oz/⅔ cup)
soft brown sugar	40 g (1½ oz/¼ cup)
unsalted butter	40 g (1½ oz), chilled and cubed
desiccated coconut	20 g (¾ oz/¼ cup)
roasted skinned hazelnuts	2 tablespoons chopped
peaches	4, sliced
caster (superfine) sugar	80 g (2¾ oz/⅓ cup)
passionfruit	3

Preheat the oven to 200°C (400°F/Gas 6). Roll out the pastry to cover the base and side of a 20 cm (8 inch), 4 cm (1½ inch) deep flan tin. Place the pastry in the tin and prick the base. Line the pastry shell with a sheet of crumpled baking paper and pour in some baking beads or uncooked rice. Bake for 15 minutes, then remove the paper and beads and return to the oven for another 6–8 minutes. Set aside to cool. Reduce the oven to 180°C (350°F/Gas 4).

Rub the flour, brown sugar and butter together. Add the coconut and chopped hazelnuts. Set aside.

Heat a frying pan over high heat. Toss the peach slices in the caster sugar. Tip the peaches into the frying pan and cook, moving them occasionally until they are evenly coated in caramel. Add the passionfruit pulp and remove the pan from the heat.

Spoon the peach mixture into the pastry case and top with the hazelnut mixture. Bake the tart for 20–25 minutes, or until the top is golden brown.

Gently rub the butter into the flour and sugar.

Add the passionfruit pulp to the caramelized peaches.

Scatter the hazelnut crumble over the top of the tart.

cherry cheesecake .... serves 8–10

EACH LAYER OF THIS CHEESECAKE JUST GETS BETTER, FROM THE BUTTERY BISCUIT BASE TO THE RICH, CREAMY MIDDLE TO THE DELICIOUSLY JUICY CHERRY TOPPING. TO REMOVE THE STONES FROM THE CHERRIES, EITHER USE A CHERRY PITTER OR CUT THE FRUIT IN HALF WITH A SMALL KNIFE, THEN REMOVE THE STONES.

cherries	540 g (1 lb 3 oz), pitted and halved
caster (superfine) sugar	125 g (4½ oz/heaped ½ cup)
lemon juice	2 tablespoons
sweet shortbread biscuits (cookies)	200 g (7 oz)
unsalted butter	90 g (3¼ oz), melted
cream cheese	500 g (1 lb 2 oz/2 cups), softened
honey	125 g (4½ oz/heaped ⅓ cup)
natural vanilla extract	2 teaspoons
lemon	1, zest finely grated
eggs	4, at room temperature
thickened (whipping) cream	200 ml (7 fl oz)

Put 100 ml (3½ fl oz) of water in a saucepan with the cherries, sugar and lemon juice. Bring to the boil, then reduce the heat to low. Cook, stirring occasionally and lightly pressing the cherries to crush them, for 12–15 minutes, or until the cherries are soft and there are 2–3 tablespoons of syrup left. Remove from the heat and set aside to cool.

Preheat the oven to 180°C (350°F/Gas 4). Lightly grease a 22 cm (8½ inch) spring-form cake tin and line the base. Crush the biscuits in a food processor until they form fine crumbs. Add the butter and process until combined. Press the mixture into the base of the prepared tin and freeze for 10 minutes. Cover the outside of the tin with strong foil to prevent any water seepage during cooking. Place the tin in a deep roasting tin.

Beat the cream cheese, honey, vanilla and lemon zest until smooth. Add the eggs, one at a time, beating well after each addition. Stir in the cream. Pour the mixture over the crumb base. Pour enough hot water into the roasting tin to come halfway up the side of the cake tin. Bake for 45 minutes, or until almost set. Carefully spoon the cherry mixture over the cheesecake, lightly spreading it to the edge. Bake for 10 minutes, or until just set. Discard the foil, place the cheesecake on a wire rack to cool in the tin, then refrigerate until ready to serve. Allow the cheesecake to return to room temperature before serving.

Cook the cherries until they are soft and syrupy.

Pour in the filling once the base is cold.

Be gentle when spreading the cherries over the cheesecake.

vanilla buttermilk panna cotta
with summer fruits . . . . serves 4

ITS NAME SEEMS TO SUGGEST OTHERWISE, BUT BUTTERMILK IS ACTUALLY MADE FROM SKIM MILK AND IS LOWER IN FAT THAN FULL-CREAM MILK. AN ACID-PRODUCING BACTERIA IS ADDED TO THE MILK, THICKENING IT AND GIVING IT A TANGY FLAVOUR. IT GOES PERFECTLY IN THIS PANNA COTTA, PRODUCING A SMOOTH, CREAMY DESSERT.

panna cotta

powdered gelatine	2 teaspoons
cream (whipping)	250 ml (9 fl oz/1 cup)
caster (superfine) sugar	55 g (2 oz/¼ cup)
vanilla bean	½, split lengthways
buttermilk	250 ml (9 fl oz/1 cup)
passionfruit	2
caster (superfine) sugar	2 teaspoons
small pineapple	½, peeled and cored
small red papaya	½, seeded and peeled

To make the panna cotta, lightly grease 4 x 125 ml (4 fl oz/½ cup) metal, glass or ceramic moulds.

Put 2 teaspoons of water in a small bowl and sprinkle with the gelatine. Leave the gelatine to sponge and swell. Put the cream, sugar and vanilla bean in a small saucepan and stir over low heat for 2–3 minutes, or until the sugar has dissolved. Whisk the gelatine mixture into the cream mixture until the gelatine has dissolved. Set aside to infuse for 3 minutes.

Scrape the seeds from the vanilla bean into the cream mixture, discarding the vanilla pod. Pour the mixture into a bowl. Shake the buttermilk carton well before measuring, then whisk the buttermilk into the cream mixture. Divide the mixture among the prepared moulds. Put the moulds on a tray, cover with plastic wrap and refrigerate for 3–4 hours, or until set.

Sieve the passionfruit pulp into a small bowl, discarding the seeds. Stir in the sugar. Cut the pineapple and papaya into long thin slivers.

To serve, gently run a small knife around the side of each mould and turn the panna cotta out onto large serving plates. If they don't readily come out, briefly dip the moulds in a bowl of hot water. Arrange the fruit slivers around the panna cotta and drizzle with the passionfruit juice.

Remove the papaya seeds using a spoon.

Divide the panna cotta mixture among the moulds.

ricotta and berry tartlets

RICOTTA IS A FRESH CHEESE THAT PROVES SURPRISINGLY ADAPTABLE IN THE KITCHEN. IN SWEET DISHES IT GOES WELL WITH CHOCOLATE, DRIED FRUIT, NUTS AND BERRIES. IT MAKES A NICE ALTERNATIVE TO A FRANGIPANE-STYLE FILLING IN THESE TARTLETS AND ALSO PROTECTS THE FRUIT DURING COOKING, ENSURING A MOIST FILLING.

pastry

plain (all-purpose) flour	150 g (5½ oz/1¼ cups)
ground almonds	35 g (1¼ oz/⅓ cup)
caster (superfine) sugar	1 tablespoon
unsalted butter	85 g (3 oz), chilled and cubed
egg yolk	1, at room temperature

filling

mixed berries, such as raspberries, strawberries and blueberries	300 g (10½ oz/2½ cups)
egg	1, at room temperature
caster (superfine) sugar	60 g (2¼ oz/¼ cup)
lemon juice	1 tablespoon
smooth ricotta cheese	150 g (5½ oz/scant ⅔ cup)
icing (confectioners') sugar	for dusting

To make the pastry, put the flour, ground almonds, sugar, butter and a pinch of salt in a food processor. Process until the mixture resembles breadcrumbs. Add the egg yolk and 1 tablespoon of cold water. Process until the mixture just forms a ball, adding a little extra water if the pastry is too dry. Turn the pastry out onto a work surface. Flatten it into a disc, cover with plastic wrap and refrigerate for 30 minutes.

Lightly grease 6 x 9 cm (3½ inch), 2 cm (¾ inch) deep tartlet tins. Roll out the pastry on a lightly floured surface to a thickness of 3 mm (⅛ inch). Cut out 6 x 13 cm (5 inch) circles and place in the tins. Prick the base of the pastry with a fork and refrigerate for 10 minutes. Preheat the oven to 200°C (400°F/Gas 6).

To make the filling, hull any strawberries and chop any larger berries. Put the egg, caster sugar and lemon juice in a heatproof bowl and place over a saucepan of simmering water, making sure the base of the bowl doesn't touch the water. Whisk with an electric whisk for 5–6 minutes, or until light and creamy. Stir in the ricotta. Divide the berries among the tartlet cases and spoon over the ricotta mixture. Bake for 20–22 minutes, or until the edges of the pastry are golden brown. Serve warm or at room temperature, dusted with icing sugar.

Hull the strawberries and chop any larger ones.

Make sure the base of the bowl doesn't touch the water.

Divide the berries evenly among the pastry cases.

autumn

If desserts can be said to help ease the passing of summer and the arrival of colder weather, then these autumn recipes are just the ones to do it. What is there to lament when figs, plums, blackberries and pears start appearing in the fruit shops, and desserts such as fig and apple pies with rosewater cream, corella pear tarte tatin and plum upside-down cake are possible? Autumn recipes, like the season itself, have their own pleasures.

This chapter contains some classic flavour combinations. Plums with almonds, blackberries with crème anglaise, and figs with hazelnuts and yoghurt are no less delicious for their familiarity. But, like every season, autumn also has its own rare treasures. Pomegranates, native to Iran and favoured by the ancient Persians and Egyptians, can be found in shops; big round red fruit filled with little jewel-like capsules of pulp and seeds. These are the sort of exotic fruit you might tend to overlook as you wonder what they taste like, and how they should be prepared. Well, two suggestions are fruit fritters with pomegranate sauce, and Turkish delight ice cream.

With the gradual dwindling of the fresh fruit selection, dried fruit becomes a useful standby. Dried fruit has its own concentrated sweetness and appealing texture to offer, and is particularly at home in fruit fritters.

The recipes in this chapter also mark a welcome return of the sweet, sticky and syrupy. Pistachio and lime semolina cake with date confit, and stem ginger cheesecake with Sauternes poached plums are desserts that encourage the licking of fingers, bowls and spoons. Freshly baked cakes and tarts, ganache logs and strudels all seem very much at home during autumn.

This chapter also shows you how to make a really good shortcrust (pie) pastry, one of the most indispensable techniques for anyone who enjoys baking. Ready-made shortcrust is available, and some brands are good, but none can provide the satisfaction and taste that come with making your own.

turkish delight ice cream . . . . serves 6

THIS SWEET, ROSE-HUED ICE CREAM WILL HAVE EVERYONE WONDERING WHAT THE SECRET ELEMENT IS. MAKE SURE YOU BUY A GOOD-QUALITY TURKISH DELIGHT. IF IT IS QUITE PALE, YOU CAN ADD A FEW DROPS OF RED FOOD COLOURING TO THE MILK AFTER DISSOLVING THE TURKISH DELIGHT.

milk	375 ml (13 fl oz/1½ cups)
cream (whipping)	500 ml (17 fl oz/2 cups)
caster (superfine) sugar	150 g (5½ oz/⅔ cup)
egg yolks	6, at room temperature
Turkish delight	100 g (3½ oz), roughly chopped
pomegranate seeds	2 tablespoons

Put 250 ml (9 fl oz/1 cup) of the milk in a saucepan with the cream and sugar. Cook over medium heat, stirring constantly for a few minutes, until the sugar has dissolved and the milk is just about to boil. Remove from the heat.

Whisk the egg yolks in a bowl for 1 minute, or until combined, then add 60 ml (2 fl oz/¼ cup) of the hot milk mixture. Stir to combine, then pour into the remaining milk mixture. Return the saucepan to low–medium heat and cook, stirring constantly with a wooden spoon, until the mixture thickens and coats the back of the spoon. Do not allow the mixture to boil. Strain through a fine sieve and set aside to cool.

Put the remaining milk and the Turkish delight in a small saucepan over medium heat. Stir constantly until the Turkish delight has dissolved into the milk. Stir into the custard mixture and set aside to cool.

Transfer the mixture to an ice-cream machine to churn and freeze according to the manufacturer's instructions. Alternatively, transfer to a shallow tray and freeze, whisking every couple of hours until frozen to give the ice cream a creamy texture.

Serve the ice cream topped with the pomegranate seeds.

Add the chopped Turkish delight to the remaining milk.

Stir over gentle heat to dissolve the Turkish delight.

blackberry and pear strudel .... serves 6–8

THANK GOODNESS FOR READY-MADE FILO PASTRY. WITHOUT IT, FEW WOULD ATTEMPT MAKING A STRUDEL. THIS VERSION BRANCHES OUT FROM THE TRADITIONAL APPLE AND RAISIN OR CHERRY AND CREAM CHEESE FILLING BY COMBINING CITRUS-INFUSED PEARS WITH BLACKBERRIES, ALMONDS AND SULTANAS.

unsalted butter	120 g (4¼ oz)
natural vanilla extract	½ teaspoon
pears	4, peeled, cored and chopped
orange zest	1 teaspoon finely grated
lemon	½, juiced
filo pastry	5 sheets
fresh breadcrumbs	120 g (4¼ oz/1½ cups)
blackberries	200 g (7 oz/1½ cups)
toasted flaked almonds	50 g (1¾ oz/½ cup)
sultanas	60 g (2¼ oz/½ cup)
caster (superfine) sugar	165 g (5¾ oz/¾ cup)
icing (confectioners') sugar	for dusting
custard or vanilla ice cream	to serve

Preheat the oven to 180°C (350°F/Gas 4) and line a baking sheet with baking paper. Melt 100 g (3½ oz) of the butter with the vanilla.

Melt the remaining butter in a frying pan and sauté the pear over low heat for 5 minutes, or until tender. Transfer to a large bowl with the orange zest and lemon juice. Toss lightly to combine.

Lay a sheet of filo pastry on a flat surface. Brush the melted butter over the pastry and sprinkle lightly with breadcrumbs. Cover with another sheet of pastry and repeat the process until you have used all the pastry. Sprinkle with the remaining breadcrumbs.

Add the blackberries, almonds, sultanas and caster sugar to the pear mixture and toss gently to combine. Shape the filling into a log along one long edge of the pastry, leaving a 5 cm (2 inch) border. Fold in the sides, then roll up and place, seam side down, on the prepared baking sheet. Brush with the remaining melted butter and bake for 40 minutes, or until golden brown. Dust with icing sugar and serve with custard or vanilla ice cream.

The pear is a risky fruit — when perfectly ripe, its juicy, mellow richness is hard to beat, but miss that brief moment, and the downward slide will have already begun. The pear's versatility in cooking makes it worth the gamble, however. Pears can be used in sweet and savoury dishes, eaten fresh in salads, or poached, puréed, baked and sautéed. Available for much of the year, they are at their best, and in greatest variety, over autumn. Popular choices include the soft and juicy beurre bosc pear; the slow-ripening, juicy packham pear; and the aromatic william (bartlett) pear, which is ideal for cooking. When buying, choose smooth, firm but not hard pears.

brown sugar cream pots
with roasted plums . . . . serves 6

THESE CARAMELIZED PLUMS MAKE A WONDERFUL FOIL TO THE UNADULTERATED SWEET CREAMINESS OF THE CUSTARD POTS. VIN SANTO, MEANING 'HOLY WINE', IS AN ITALIAN DESSERT WINE THAT IS SMOOTH, HIGH IN ALCOHOL AND INTENSELY FLAVOURED. IF YOU CANNOT FIND VIN SANTO, USE SWEET MARSALA.

eggs	2, at room temperature
egg yolks	2, at room temperature
cream (whipping)	250 ml (9 fl oz/1 cup)
natural vanilla extract	1 teaspoon
milk	250 ml (9 fl oz/1 cup)
soft brown sugar	165 g (5¾ oz/¾ cup firmly packed)
plums	6, halved, stones removed
Vin Santo	2 tablespoons
caster (superfine) sugar	1 tablespoon

Preheat the oven to 150°C (300°F/Gas 2).

Whisk the eggs, egg yolks, cream and vanilla in a heatproof bowl until combined. Stir the milk and brown sugar in a small saucepan over low heat until the sugar has dissolved. Heat until almost boiling, then remove from the heat. Add 60 ml (2 fl oz/¼ cup) of the hot milk to the egg mixture and whisk to combine, then whisk in the remaining milk mixture.

Strain the mixture into a container with a pouring lip and pour into 6 x 125 ml (4 fl oz/½ cup) ovenproof ramekins. Put the ramekins in a deep roasting tin and pour enough boiling water into the roasting tin to come halfway up the sides of the ramekins. Bake for 45 minutes, or until set. Set aside to cool for 30 minutes.

Meanwhile, increase the oven to 200°C (400°F/Gas 6). Arrange the plums on a baking tray in a single layer, cut side up. Drizzle with the Vin Santo and sprinkle with the caster sugar. Roast for 12 minutes, or until the plums soften and the skin blisters. Cool to room temperature, then serve alongside the cream pots.

Whisk the hot milk into the egg mixture until combined.

Drizzle the Vin Santo over the cut side of the plums.

Roast until the plums soften and the skin blisters.

fruit fritters with pomegranate sauce .... serves 8

THIS SOPHISTICATED DESSERT IS A FAR CRY FROM THE HUMBLE BANANA FRITTER WITH ICE CREAM. IN THIS VERSION, FRUIT AND NUTS ARE SOAKED IN RUM, WHILE THE BATTER INCORPORATES LEMON ZEST, VANILLA AND WHITE WINE. TO FINISH, RUBY RED POMEGRANATE SAUCE IS SET ASIDE TO BE DRIZZLED LUXURIANTLY OVER THE TOP.

apples	3
rum	1 tablespoon
toasted slivered almonds	40 g (1 1/2 oz/1/3 cup)
dried apricots	40 g (1 1/2 oz/1/4 cup)
raisins	40 g (1 1/2 oz/1/3 cup)
ground cinnamon	1/4 teaspoon
oil	for deep-frying
icing (confectioners') sugar	for sprinkling

batter

plain (all-purpose) flour	220 g (7 3/4 oz/1 3/4 cups)
caster (superfine) sugar	2 tablespoons
dry white wine	250 ml (9 fl oz/1 cup)
olive oil	1 tablespoon
lemon zest	1 teaspoon finely grated
natural vanilla extract	1 teaspoon
eggs	3, at room temperature, separated

sauce

sugar	70 g (2 1/2 oz/1/3 cup)
pomegranates	2
lemon juice	2 teaspoons

Peel, quarter and core the apples, then thinly slice and roughly chop them. Put the apple in a large bowl and toss with the rum. Chop the almonds and apricots and add to the apple. Add the raisins and cinnamon and toss to combine. Set aside for 1 hour.

Meanwhile, to make the batter, sift the flour into a bowl and add the sugar. Gradually stir in the wine and olive oil. Add the lemon zest, vanilla and egg yolks and beat to a smooth batter. Set aside in a cool place for 50 minutes.

To make the sauce, put the sugar and 250 ml (9 fl oz/1 cup) of water in a small saucepan. Bring to the boil and cook for about 15 minutes, or until reduced by half. Scrape the seeds and squeeze the juice from the pomegranates into a bowl. Discard the white pith. Purée the pomegranate seeds and juice in a food processor, then pass the mixture through a coarse strainer. You should have about 100 ml (3 1/2 fl oz) of liquid. Add the liquid and the lemon juice to the saucepan containing the sugar syrup and simmer for 5 minutes. Remove from the heat and set aside.

Fold the apple mixture through the batter. Whisk the egg whites until stiff peaks form. Using a metal spoon, fold a large scoop of egg whites through the batter, then lightly fold the remaining egg whites through the batter.

Fill a deep-fryer or medium saucepan one-third full with oil. Heat the oil to 160°C (315°F), or until a cube of bread dropped into the oil turns golden in 30 seconds. Carefully drop heaped tablespoons of the batter into the oil and fry for about 1 minute, or until golden. Remove with tongs and drain on paper towels.

Sprinkle the fritters with icing sugar and serve immediately with the pomegranate sauce for drizzling over the top.

Add the zest, vanilla and yolks, then beat to a smooth batter.

Make sure you don't include any of the white pith.

plum and biscotti ice cream .... serves 4

FOR THE GREATEST VISUAL IMPACT, USE LOVELY DARK-FLESHED BLOOD PLUMS, RATHER THAN YELLOW-FLESHED ONES. THE DARK VARIETIES TEND TO BE BETTER FOR COOKING. CHOP THE BISCOTTI THOROUGHLY — THEIR CRUNCHINESS SHOULD BE PART OF THE ICE CREAM, NOT A SEPARATE ELEMENT TO CONTEND WITH.

plums	450 g (1 lb)
caster (superfine) sugar	80 g (2¾ oz/⅓ cup)
almond extract	a few drops
good-quality ready-made custard	500 ml (17 fl oz/2 cups)
almond biscotti	80 g (2¾ oz), chopped

Halve the plums, removing the stones. Combine the sugar and 125 ml (4 fl oz/½ cup) of water in a saucepan. Add the plums and poach for 10 minutes. Set aside to cool.

Purée the plums, poaching liquid and almond extract until smooth. Carefully stir the plum mixture into the custard. Pour the mixture into a shallow plastic container and freeze for 1–1½ hours, or until the sides and base have frozen and the centre is a soft slush.

Using a hand blender or electric whisk, blend or beat the plum mixture until it is uniformly slushy. Return the mixture to the freezer, repeating the blending process at least twice.

Stir in the biscotti and freeze for another 30–60 minutes, or until the ice cream is firm.

After the heady rush of summer fruits, plums can sometimes struggle for attention, though undeservedly so. They are particularly valuable for cooks, who can use them in savoury and sweet dishes, preserves and jams. Plums are also excellent for poaching and stewing. Native to Europe and North America, there are over 2000 varieties grown worldwide. The flesh can be yellow or dark purple, the flavour tart or sweet. Tart varieties, particularly the blood plums, are best used in cooking; sweeter and juicier ones should be enjoyed fresh. When buying plums, look for pleasantly scented fruit that yield slightly when pressed, and have a whitish bloom on the skin.

pistachio and lime semolina cake with date glaze .... serves 16

THIS CAKE TAKES ITS CUE FROM THE COOKING OF THE EASTERN MEDITERRANEAN, WHERE SEMOLINA-BASED CAKES AND PASTRIES ARE OFTEN SOAKED IN SWEET SYRUPS. DATES ARE A POPULAR CHOICE FOR SUCH SYRUPS, DUE TO THEIR HIGH SUGAR CONTENT. TO EASE THE RICHNESS OF THE SYRUP, LIME JUICE HAS BEEN ADDED.

date glaze

caster (superfine) sugar	185 g (6$^1/_2$ oz/heaped $^3/_4$ cup)
pitted dates	200 g (7 oz/1$^1/_4$ cups) roughly chopped
limes	2, juiced
unsalted butter	125 g (4$^1/_2$ oz), softened
caster (superfine) sugar	125 g (4$^1/_2$ oz/heaped $^1/_2$ cup)
limes	2, zest finely grated
eggs	2, at room temperature
fine semolina	360 g (12$^3/_4$ oz/3 cups)
pistachio nuts	90 g (3$^1/_4$ oz/$^2/_3$ cup) chopped
baking powder	2 teaspoons
bicarbonate of soda (baking soda)	$^1/_2$ teaspoon
plain yoghurt	185 g (6$^1/_2$ oz/$^3/_4$ cup)
milk	125 ml (4 fl oz/$^1/_2$ cup)
crème fraîche or thick (double/heavy) cream	to serve

To make the date glaze, put the sugar in a small saucepan with 185 ml (6 fl oz/$^3/_4$ cup) of water. Stir over medium heat until the sugar has dissolved. Add the dates and lime juice and bring to the boil. Reduce the heat and simmer for 6–8 minutes, or until the dates have softened. Remove from the heat and set aside to cool.

Preheat the oven to 180°C (350°F/Gas 4). Grease and line a 23 cm (9 inch) square cake tin.

Put the butter, sugar and lime zest in a large bowl and beat with electric beaters until light and fluffy. Add the eggs, one at a time, beating well after each addition. In a separate bowl, combine the semolina, pistachios, baking powder and bicarbonate of soda. Stir the semolina mixture and yoghurt alternately through the butter mixture, then stir in the milk. Pour the mixture into the prepared tin and bake for 40 minutes, or until a skewer comes out clean when inserted into the centre of the cake.

Spoon the date glaze over the hot cake in the tin and place on a wire rack to cool. Serve the cake warm or at room temperature, accompanied by crème fraîche or thick cream.

Cook the chopped dates until they soften.

Mix the chopped pistachio nuts into the semolina.

Stir the semolina mixture and yoghurt into the butter mixture.

fig and apple pies
with rosewater cream...serves 4

THESE LITTLE PIES ARE A REAL CELEBRATION OF AUTUMN, WITH FIGS, APPLES, CITRUS, CINNAMON AND VANILLA
ALL COMBINING TO PRODUCE A VERY WARMING, COMFORTING FLAVOUR —— A WONDERFUL WAY TO END A MEAL.
THE PIES CAN BE PREPARED AHEAD OF TIME AND REFRIGERATED UNTIL IT IS TIME TO PUT THEM IN THE OVEN.

rosewater cream

thickened (whipping) cream	125 ml (4 fl oz/1/2 cup)
rosewater	2 teaspoons
caster (superfine) sugar	1 tablespoon
apples	3, peeled, cored and cut into 2 cm (3/4 inch) cubes
figs	3 fresh or 6 semi-dried, cut into 2 cm (3/4 inch) cubes
unsalted butter	40 g (11/2 oz)
caster (superfine) sugar	60 g (21/4 oz/1/4 cup)
orange	1, zest grated
lemon	1, zest grated
lemon	1/2, juiced
cinnamon stick	1
natural vanilla extract	1 teaspoon
ready-made shortcrust (pie) pastry	1 sheet
egg white	1, at room temperature, beaten

To make the rosewater cream, beat the cream, rosewater and sugar in a bowl until thick. Refrigerate until needed.

Put the apple, figs, butter, sugar, orange zest, lemon zest, lemon juice, cinnamon stick, vanilla and 2 tablespoons of water in a saucepan. Stir over high heat until the butter has melted and the sugar has dissolved. Bring to the boil, then reduce the heat and simmer for 10 minutes, or until the apple is soft. Remove from the heat and set aside to cool.

Preheat the oven to 180°C (350°F/Gas 4) and lightly grease 4 x 125 ml (4 fl oz/1/2 cup) ovenproof ramekins.

Pour the cooled apple mixture into the ramekins, discarding the cinnamon stick. Cut out four rounds of pastry 1 cm (1/2 inch) wider than the diameter of the ramekins. Lay the pastry rounds over the ramekins, pressing around the rims to seal. Brush the pastry with the egg white. Bake the pies for 40 minutes, or until golden brown. Serve warm with the rosewater cream.

Figs have been found among the funerary treasures in ancient Egyptian tombs, grew in the Hanging Gardens of Babylon, were regarded as a symbol of fertility by the ancient Greeks and appeared in the Bible. All in all, figs have long been held in high regard. Small, soft and pear-shaped, varying in colour from pale green to purple, the fruit has sweet, pulpy flesh full of tiny edible seeds. In cooking, figs are poached, grilled (broiled), added to tarts and preserved. The stems should always be removed before cooking. When buying, select firm, unblemished fruit that yield to gentle pressure. Figs are also sold semi-dried and dried.

three ways with almonds

ALMONDS ARE OFTEN IN THE BACKGROUND, A SUPPORTING FLAVOUR ONLY, SO IT'S NICE TO SEE THEM SHINE IN THEIR OWN RIGHT OCCASIONALLY. FOR THE BEST FLAVOUR, PREPARE ALMONDS YOURSELF. TO BLANCH, POUR BOILING WATER OVER THE NUTS, SOAK FOR 2 MINUTES, THEN SLIP THE SKINS OFF WITH YOUR FINGERS. CHOP THE NUTS WHILE THEY ARE STILL WARM. TO ROAST, PUT THE NUTS ON A TRAY AND COOK FOR 8–10 MINUTES IN A 180°C (350°F/GAS 4) OVEN, THEN GRIND IN A FOOD PROCESSOR OR USING A MORTAR AND PESTLE.

almond brownies

Melt 200 g (7 oz/1 1/3 cups) chopped dark couverture chocolate in a heatproof bowl over a saucepan of simmering water. Remove from the heat and set aside to cool for 5 minutes. Beat 125 g (4 1/2 oz) softened unsalted butter and 115 g (4 oz/1/2 cup) caster (superfine) sugar with electric beaters for 10 minutes. Add 2 eggs, one at a time, beating until well combined. Sift together 2 tablespoons Dutch cocoa powder, 30 g (1 oz/1/4 cup) plain (all-purpose) flour and 30 g (1 oz/1/4 cup) self-raising flour in a separate bowl. Stir the cocoa mixture into the butter mixture until combined. Stir in the melted chocolate. Pour the mixture into a lined 20 cm (8 inch), 5 cm (2 inch) deep square cake tin and neatly arrange 80 g (2 3/4 oz/1/2 cup) blanched almonds over the surface. Bake in a preheated 170°C (325°F/Gas 3) oven for 35 minutes. Set aside to cool in the tin for 5 minutes before transferring to a wire rack to cool completely. Cut the brownies into 4 cm (1 1/2 inch) squares and dust with cocoa powder. Makes 25.

caramelized almond tarts

Roast 50 g (1 3/4 oz/1/2 cup) flaked almonds in a preheated 200°C (400°F/Gas 6) oven for 7 minutes, or until golden. Put 60 g (2 1/4 oz) unsalted butter, 80 g (2 3/4 oz/1/3 cup firmly packed) soft brown sugar and 60 ml (2 fl oz/1/4 cup) water in a frying pan and stir over low heat until the sugar has dissolved. Stir in the almonds, then divide the mixture among 4 x 9 cm (3 1/2 inch) greased loose-based tart tins. Thaw 1 sheet of frozen puff pastry and cut it into 4 x 9 cm (3 1/2 inch) rounds. Place the pastry rounds on the tops of the tart tins and bake for 10 minutes, or until puffed and golden. Immediately turn the tarts out of the tins so the pastry is on the bottom. Set aside to cool. Serves 4.

almond and lime puddings

Put 115 g (4 oz/1/2 cup) caster (superfine) sugar, 20 g (3/4 oz) unsalted butter and 60 ml (2 fl oz/1/4 cup) lime juice in a small saucepan. Stir over low heat until the sugar has dissolved. Bring to a simmer, then cook, without stirring, for 3 minutes, or until syrupy. Divide the syrup among 4 x 150 ml (5 fl oz) ovenproof bowls. Sift 125 g (4 1/2 oz/1 cup) icing (confectioners') sugar, 60 g (2 1/4 oz/1/2 cup) plain (all-purpose) flour and 1/4 teaspoon baking powder into a bowl and stir in 70 g (2 1/2 oz/2/3 cup) ground almonds. Add 3 egg whites, 1 teaspoon natural vanilla extract, 2 teaspoons finely grated lime zest and 80 g (2 3/4 oz) melted unsalted butter and stir to combine. Divide the mixture among the bowls. Bake the puddings in a preheated 160°C (315°F/Gas 2–3) oven for 20–22 minutes, or until golden. Set aside to cool for 10 minutes before serving warm with thick (double/heavy) cream. Serves 4.

almond brownies

plum and almond tart..serves 8

THE PLEASURE IN THIS TART IS AS MUCH IN THE MAKING AS IN THE EATING. IT DOESN'T MATTER IF YOUR PASTRY IS NOT FLAWLESSLY BUTTERY AND SMOOTH, OR YOUR PLUMS AREN'T PERFECTLY PLACED, THE RESULT WILL BE THE SAME — A DELICIOUS COMBINATION OF FRUIT AND NUTS.

pastry

plain (all-purpose) flour	185 g (6½ oz/1½ cups)
unsalted butter	150 g (5½ oz), chilled and cubed
caster (superfine) sugar	55 g (2 oz/¼ cup)
sour cream	1 tablespoon

filling

unsalted butter	125 g (4½ oz), softened
caster (superfine) sugar	115 g (4 oz/½ cup)
eggs	2, at room temperature
ground almonds	100 g (3½ oz/1 cup)
plain (all-purpose) flour	2 tablespoons
plums	8–10, halved, stones removed
cream or ice cream	to serve

To make the pastry, put the flour, butter and sugar in a food processor and process in short bursts until the mixture resembles fine breadcrumbs. Add the sour cream and process in short bursts until the mixture comes together in a ball. Cover with plastic wrap and refrigerate for 20 minutes.

Preheat the oven to 200°C (400°F/Gas 6) and grease a 23 cm (9 inch), 2 cm (¾ inch) deep loose-based flan tin.

Roll out the pastry to a thickness of 3 mm (⅛ inch) and use it to line the tin. Prick the pastry base with a fork and refrigerate for 30 minutes. Line the pastry shell with a sheet of crumpled baking paper and pour in some baking beads or uncooked rice. Bake for 15 minutes, remove the paper and beads and return to the oven for another 5–7 minutes to ensure the pastry is crisp. Set aside to cool. Reduce the oven to 180°C (350°F/Gas 4).

To make the filling, cream the butter and sugar with electric beaters until light and fluffy. Add the eggs, one at a time, beating well after each addition. Fold in the ground almonds and flour. Spread the almond mixture over the base of the pastry case and top with the plum halves, cut side down. Bake for 25–30 minutes, or until the filling is set and golden. Serve the tart warm or at room temperature with cream or ice cream.

Add the ground almonds after the eggs have been incorporated.

Spread the filling evenly into the pastry shell.

Arrange the plums, cut side down, on the almond filling.

chocolate ganache log......................................serves 8–10

A GANACHE IS BASICALLY A FOOLISHLY RICH ICING (FROSTING) MADE OF CHOCOLATE AND CREAM. THE TWO ARE HEATED UNTIL THE CHOCOLATE HAS MELTED, THEN THE MIXTURE IS COOLED AND SPREAD OVER A CAKE. THIS DESSERT IS NOTHING IF NOT INDULGENT, AND DESERVES TO BE APPROACHED WITH GUSTO.

cake

unsalted butter	200 g (7 oz), softened
caster (superfine) sugar	150 g (5½ oz/⅔ cup)
eggs	6, at room temperature, separated
ground almonds	125 g (4½ oz/1¼ cups)
dark chocolate	150 g (5½ oz/1 cup) chopped, melted

ganache

cream (whipping)	150 ml (5 fl oz)
dark chocolate	225 g (8 oz/1½ cups) chopped
instant coffee granules	2 teaspoons

To make the cake, preheat the oven to 180°C (350°F/Gas 4). Grease and line a 25 x 30 cm (10 x 12 inch) Swiss roll tin (jelly roll tin).

Beat the butter and sugar with electric beaters until light and fluffy. Add the egg yolks, one at a time, beating well after each addition. Stir in the ground almonds and melted chocolate. Beat the egg whites in a separate bowl until stiff peaks form, then gently fold into the chocolate mixture.

Spread the mixture into the prepared tin and bake for 15 minutes. Reduce the oven to 160°C (315°F/Gas 2–3) and bake for another 30–35 minutes, or until a skewer comes out clean when inserted into the centre of the cake. Turn the cake onto a wire rack to cool.

To make the ganache, put the cream and chopped chocolate in a heatproof bowl over a small saucepan of barely simmering water, making sure the base of the bowl doesn't touch the water. Stir occasionally until the mixture is melted and combined. Stir in the coffee until it has dissolved. Remove from the heat and set aside to cool for 2 hours, or until thickened to a spreading consistency.

Cut the cake lengthways into three even pieces. Place a piece of cake on a serving plate and spread with a layer of ganache. Top with another layer of cake and another layer of ganache, followed by the remaining cake. Refrigerate for 30 minutes to set slightly. Cover the top and sides of the log with the remaining ganache and refrigerate for 3 hours, or preferably overnight.

Stir the ground almonds and chocolate into the cake mixture.

Spread the batter evenly into the prepared tin.

baked yoghurt tart with figs and hazelnuts

serves 6–8

UNLIKE MANY TARTS THAT USE NUTS, BUTTER AND FLOUR FOR THEIR FILLING, THIS MEDITERRANEAN-INSPIRED RECIPE FEATURES YOGHURT AND A HIGHER PROPORTION OF EGGS THAN NORMAL TO ENSURE A MOIST, SMOOTH TEXTURE. THE SLIGHTLY SHARP FLAVOUR OF THE FILLING IS THE IDEAL CONTRAST TO THE RICH, SWEET FIGS.

pastry

plain (all-purpose) flour	150 g (5 1/2 oz/1 1/4 cups)
ground hazelnuts	80 g (2 3/4 oz/3/4 cup)
unsalted butter	90 g (3 1/4 oz), cubed
egg yolk	1, at room temperature

filling

eggs	3, at room temperature
egg yolks	2, at room temperature
caster (superfine) sugar	125 g (4 1/2 oz/heaped 1/2 cup)
vanilla beans	2, split lengthways
Greek-style yoghurt	200 g (7 oz/heaped 3/4 cup)
cornflour (cornstarch)	30 g (1 oz/1/4 cup)
plain (all-purpose) flour	30 g (1 oz/1/4 cup)
figs	7, sliced
roasted skinned hazelnuts	100 g (3 1/2 oz/heaped 3/4 cup) roughly chopped
whipped cream	to serve

To make the pastry, put the flour, ground hazelnuts, butter and a pinch of salt in a food processor and process until the mixture resembles breadcrumbs. Add the egg yolk and 1 tablespoon of cold water. Process until the mixture just forms a ball, adding a little extra water if the dough is too dry. Turn out onto a work surface and flatten into a disc. Cover with plastic wrap and refrigerate for 30 minutes.

Preheat the oven to 180°C (350°F/Gas 4). Lightly grease a 23 cm (9 inch) shallow tart tin. Roll out the pastry on a lightly floured surface until 3 mm (1/8 inch) thick. Carefully transfer the pastry into the tin, prick the base with a fork and refrigerate for 10 minutes. Roll a rolling pin across the top of the tart tin to remove any excess pastry.

To make the filling, beat the eggs, egg yolks and sugar in a bowl until the sugar has dissolved. Scrape the seeds from the vanilla beans into the egg mixture and stir in the yoghurt. Combine the cornflour and plain flour and lightly fold through the yoghurt mixture. Pour into the pastry case and top with the sliced figs and chopped hazelnuts. Bake for 18–20 minutes, or until just set. Leave the tart to cool in the tin, then remove and serve at room temperature. Serve with whipped cream.

Beat the eggs and sugar together until the sugar dissolves.

Pour the yoghurt filling into the pastry case.

Arrange the sliced figs and hazelnuts on top of the filling.

plum upside-down cake .... serves 8

INVERTING A CAKE ALWAYS HAS A CERTAIN SENSE OF DRAMA TO IT — THAT MOMENT OF ANTICIPATION BEFORE YOU SEE HOW IT TURNED OUT. IF YOU ARE HAVING TROUBLE REMOVING THE PLUM FLESH FROM THE STONES, SIMPLY CUT IT AWAY IN SEGMENTS.

plums	450 g (1 lb)
dark muscovado sugar	30 g (1 oz/^{1}/$_4$ cup)
unsalted butter	100 g (3^1/$_2$ oz), softened
caster (superfine) sugar	250 g (9 oz/1 heaped cup)
eggs	4, at room temperature
natural vanilla extract	1 teaspoon
orange	1, zest grated
cardamom pods	6, seeds removed and crushed
plain (all-purpose) flour	150 g (5^1/$_2$ oz/1^1/$_4$ cups)
ground almonds	150 g (5^1/$_2$ oz/1^1/$_2$ cups)
baking powder	2 teaspoons
thick (double/heavy) cream	to serve

Preheat the oven to 180°C (350°F/Gas 4), and grease and line a 23 cm (9 inch) spring-form cake tin.

Halve the plums, removing the stones. Sprinkle the muscovado sugar over the base of the prepared tin and arrange the plums, cut side down, over the sugar.

Cream the butter and caster sugar with electric beaters until light and fluffy. Add the eggs, one at a time, beating well after each addition. Add the vanilla, orange zest, crushed cardamom seeds, flour, ground almonds and baking powder. Spoon over the plums and smooth the surface with a spatula.

Bake for 50 minutes, or until a skewer comes out clean when inserted into the centre of the cake. Set aside to cool for 5 minutes before turning the cake out onto a plate. Serve with thick cream.

Like many spices, cardamom retains the appeal of the exotic though it is now readily available. Chewed by ancient Egyptians as a breath freshener, and introduced to Scandinavia by Viking traders, the plant is, in fact, native to India and Sri Lanka. The pods, the plant's dried fruit, contain the prized seeds: pungent and aromatic with a warm, sweet flavour. Beware of 'false' cardamoms: the Indian green pods are the ones to buy. Not surprisingly, Indian cooks make good use of cardamom, though the spice is also much used in the Middle East, especially as a flavouring for coffee. The pods can be used whole, and the seeds whole or ground.

milk chocolate and pecan ice cream.......... serves 6–8

A CREAMY CHOCOLATE ICE CREAM DOESN'T REALLY NEED ANY MORE CHOCOLATE BUT THESE CURLS ARE DECORATIVE AND FUN TO MAKE, SO WHY NOT? IF YOU GET A BIT CARRIED AWAY AND FIND YOU HAVE MORE CURLS THAN YOU NEED, YOU CAN STORE THEM IN AN AIRTIGHT CONTAINER — OR, OF COURSE, EAT THEM!

milk	125 ml (4 fl oz/½ cup)
vanilla bean	1, split lengthways
thickened (whipping) cream	375 ml (13 fl oz/1½ cups)
caster (superfine) sugar	90 g (3¼ oz/heaped ⅓ cup)
milk chocolate	125 g (4½ oz/1 cup) grated
egg yolks	2, at room temperature
pecans	50 g (1¾ oz/½ cup), chopped
dark chocolate	150 g (5½ oz) block

Put the milk in a heavy-based saucepan. Scrape the seeds from the vanilla bean into the saucepan and add the pod. Add 125 ml (4 fl oz/½ cup) of the cream and heat gently until just below boiling point. Add the sugar and grated milk chocolate and stir, without boiling, until smooth.

Put the egg yolks in a heatproof bowl and beat to combine. Add the cream mixture, stirring constantly. Place the bowl over a saucepan of simmering water, making sure the base of the bowl doesn't touch the water. Stir for about 20 minutes, or until the custard is thick enough to coat the back of a spoon. Strain the custard into a 750 ml (26 fl oz/3 cup) plastic or metal container and chill for 30 minutes.

Whip the remaining cream until soft peaks form, then fold the cream through the custard. Freeze for 1½–2 hours, or until the ice cream starts to set. Whisk well with electric beaters to break up the ice crystals, then return to the freezer until the ice cream begins to freeze. Beat well, then stir in the pecans. Freeze until the ice cream is set.

Scrape a vegetable peeler along the chocolate block to make dark chocolate curls. Set aside until ready to serve.

Transfer the ice cream to the refrigerator 5–10 minutes before serving. Scoop the ice cream into serving bowls and top with the chocolate curls.

Stir the chocolate and sugar into the cream until smooth.

Use a vegetable peeler to make chocolate curls.

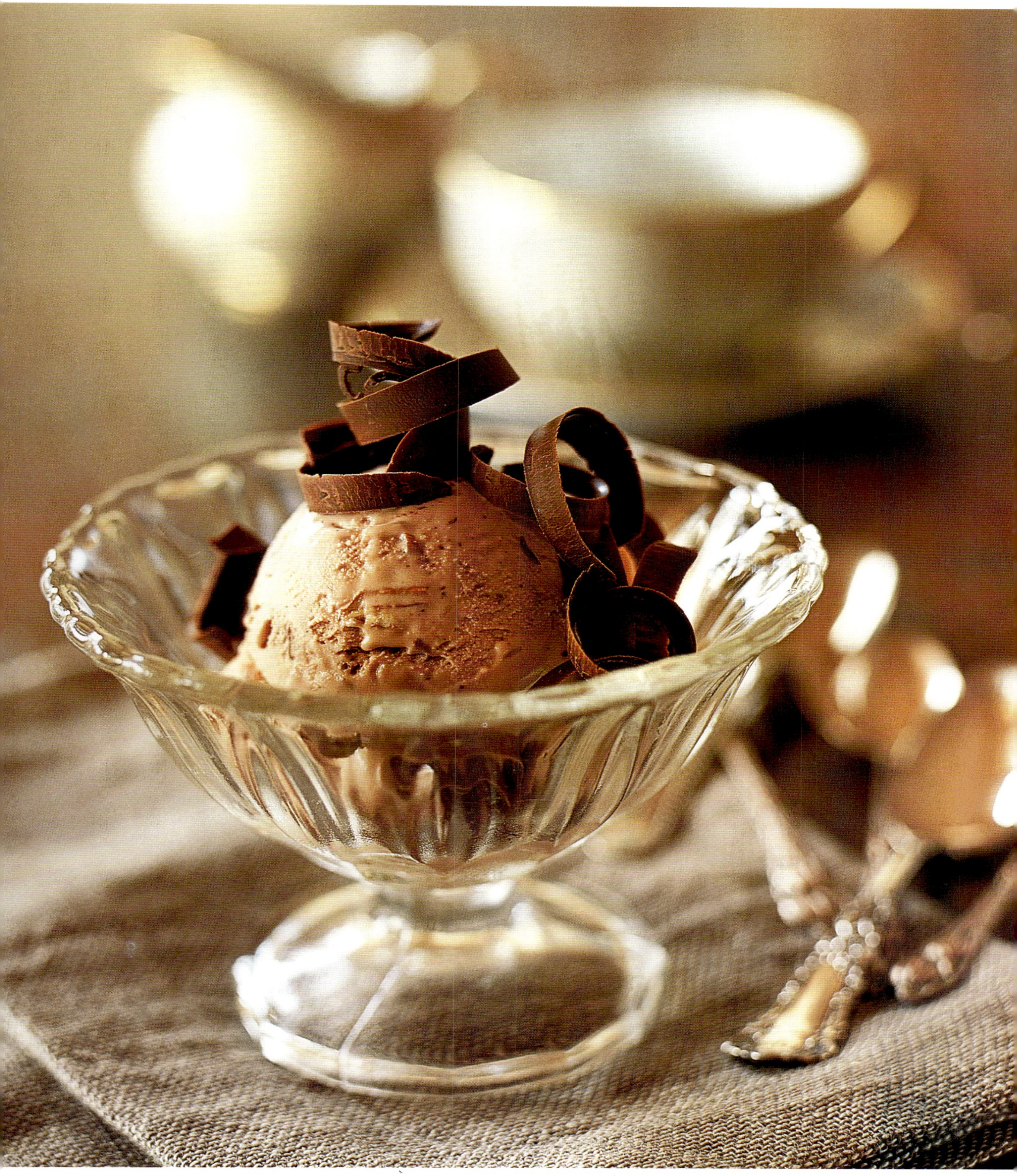

steamed blackberry puddings with crème anglaise

.... serves 8

THE KEY TO A SILKY-SMOOTH CRÈME ANGLAISE IS PATIENCE, AND THESE COMFORTING PUDDINGS PROVIDE A GOOD OPPORTUNITY TO PRACTISE. SLOWLY WHISK THE MILK INTO THE EGG YOLKS, AND SLOWLY COOK THE CUSTARD OVER LOW HEAT. WHEN DONE, SET THE CUSTARD OVER A BOWL OF ICED WATER TO PREVENT FURTHER COOKING.

unsalted butter	125 g (4^1/$_2$ oz), softened
caster (superfine) sugar	125 g (4^1/$_2$ oz/heaped ^{1}/$_2$ cup)
eggs	2, at room temperature
self-raising flour	125 g (4^1/$_2$ oz/1 cup), sifted
milk	2 tablespoons
blackberries	250 g (9 oz/2^1/$_4$ cups)

crème anglaise

milk	325 ml (11 fl oz)
egg yolks	4, at room temperature
caster (superfine) sugar	80 g (2^3/$_4$ oz/^{1}/$_3$ cup)

Preheat the oven to 180°C (350°F/Gas 4) and grease 8 x 125 ml (4 fl oz/^{1}/$_2$ cup) dariole moulds.

Using electric beaters, cream the butter and sugar together until light and fluffy. Add the eggs, one at time, beating well after each addition. Gently fold in the sifted flour and enough milk to form a dropping consistency.

Cover the base of each of the prepared moulds with a layer of blackberries. Spoon enough of the pudding mixture over the berries so that the moulds are three-quarters full. Cover the moulds with foil, sealing tightly. Place the puddings in a roasting tin and pour in enough hot water to come halfway up the sides of the moulds. Bake for 30–35 minutes, or until the puddings spring back when lightly touched.

Meanwhile, to make the crème anglaise, heat the milk to just below boiling point, then set aside. Beat the egg yolks and sugar with electric beaters until thick and pale. Slowly whisk in the hot milk and pour the mixture into a saucepan. Cook over low heat, stirring constantly for 5–7 minutes, or until the custard is thick enough to coat the back of a spoon. Remove from the heat.

To serve, unmould the puddings onto plates and drizzle with the crème anglaise.

Only fill the moulds three-quarters full.

Pour boiling water into the roasting tin around the moulds.

passionfruit polenta cake

serves 8–10

POLENTA, MADE FROM CORNMEAL, ADDS A WONDERFUL GOLDEN HUE TO THIS CAKE. COMBINED WITH THE FLOUR AND ALMONDS, IT PROVIDES A GOOD CONTRAST FOR THE SHARPER CITRUS AND PASSIONFRUIT FLAVOURS. YOU WILL NEED ABOUT SIX LARGE PASSIONFRUIT FOR THIS RECIPE.

eggs	6, at room temperature, separated
caster (superfine) sugar	150 g (5 1/2 oz/2/3 cup)
oranges	2, zest grated
passionfruit pulp	125 ml (4 fl oz/1/2 cup)
natural vanilla extract	2 teaspoons
toasted slivered almonds	150 g (5 1/2 oz/1 1/4 cups)
fine polenta	150 g (5 1/2 oz/1 cup)
self-raising flour	150 g (5 1/2 oz/1 1/4 cups)
whipped cream	to serve

syrup

oranges	2, zested and juiced
passionfruit	2
orange blossom honey	90 g (3 1/4 oz/1/4 cup)

whisky butter sauce

honey	90 g (3 1/4 oz/1/4 cup)
whisky	60 ml (2 fl oz/1/4 cup)
unsalted butter	50 g (1 3/4 oz), chilled and cubed

Preheat the oven to 170°C (325°F/Gas 3) and grease a 24 cm (9 1/2 inch) spring-form cake tin.

Whisk the egg whites in a large bowl until stiff peaks form. Beat the egg yolks and sugar in a separate bowl for 3–4 minutes, or until smooth and pale. Add the orange zest, passionfruit pulp and vanilla and beat for 15 seconds, or until smooth.

Put the almonds in a food processor and process until finely ground. Add the polenta and flour and process in short bursts until combined.

Using a metal spoon, lightly fold a large scoop of egg whites through the passionfruit mixture, then gently fold the passionfruit mixture through the remaining egg whites. Fold in the almond mixture and spoon into the prepared tin. Bake for 30–35 minutes, or until a skewer inserted into the centre of the cake comes out hot and clean. Set aside to cool for 15 minutes, then turn out onto a wire rack to cool for at least 1 hour.

To make the syrup, put the orange zest, orange juice, passionfruit pulp and honey in a small saucepan. Bring to the boil over medium heat, then reduce the heat and simmer for 5 minutes.

Transfer the cake to a serving plate with a lip, and pierce it several times with a thin metal skewer. Pour about one-quarter of the hot syrup all over the top, then add the rest once it is absorbed. Set aside for 1 hour.

To make the whisky butter sauce, put the honey and whisky in a saucepan and bring to the boil over low–medium heat. Reduce the heat and simmer for 1 minute, then gradually add the butter, one cube at a time, waiting for each cube to melt before adding the next.

Serve the cake cut into wedges, with lightly whipped cream and the whisky butter sauce.

Don't knock out the air when folding in the passionfruit mixture.

Allow the syrup to be absorbed before adding more.

the perfect shortcrust pastry

Shortcrust (pie) pastry is made using flour, fat and water and can be enriched with egg yolk to give a pastry that is softer and not as crisp. It's important to use just enough liquid to hold the pastry together — too wet and it may toughen and shrink on baking, too dry and it will be crumbly.

The secret to the perfect shortcrust pastry is to work quickly and lightly, with cool ingredients in a cool room. A cold marble slab is the ideal work surface, but if you don't have one, try resting a tray of ice cubes on your work surface for a few minutes before you start.

Sift 185 g (6½ oz/1½ cups) plain (all-purpose) flour into a large bowl and add 100 g (3½ oz) chilled, cubed unsalted butter. Using your fingertips, rub the butter into the flour until the mixture is crumb-like. Make a well in the centre, add 2–4 tablespoons of cold water and use a flat-bladed knife to mix to a soft, but not sticky, dough. Use a cutting rather than a stirring motion and turn the bowl with your free hand. To test if the dough needs more water, pinch a little dough between your fingers — if it doesn't hold together, add a little more water.

Gently gather the dough together and transfer to a floured work surface or sheet of baking paper. Gently press the dough into a ball, using a few light actions. Press into a flat disc, wrap in plastic and refrigerate for 20 minutes.

Roll out the pastry on a lightly floured work surface or between two sheets of baking paper, rolling from the centre outwards and rotating the pastry, rather than rolling backwards and forwards. If rolling on a work surface, roll the pastry around the rolling pin and lift it into the tin. If using baking paper, peel off the top sheet, then carefully invert the pastry over the tin, making sure it is centred, and peel off the bottom sheet of paper. Once the pastry is in the tin, quickly lift up the sides so they don't break on the edges of the tin. Gently ease and press the pastry into the tin. Refrigerate for at least 15 minutes to relax the pastry to prevent or minimize shrinkage, then roll a rolling pin across the top of the tin to cut off any excess pastry. Makes enough pastry to line a 23 cm (9 inch) tin.

black and white chocolate tart .... serves 12

THIS DECADENT DESSERT IS UNDOUBTEDLY ONE FOR SPECIAL OCCASIONS. HAPPILY, THE BULK OF THE WORK MUST BE DONE THE DAY BEFORE THE TART IS NEEDED, WHICH WILL FORCE YOU TO BE WELL PREPARED! RICH, CREAMY AND SUPER CHOCOLATY, IT MIGHT BE WISE TO SERVE THIS TART WITH COFFEE.

pastry

unsalted butter	90 g (3¼ oz), at room temperature
caster (superfine) sugar	55 g (2 oz/¼ cup)
egg	1, at room temperature, lightly beaten
plain (all-purpose) flour	185 g (6½ oz/1½ cups)
self-raising flour	30 g (1 oz/¼ cup)
cocoa powder	1 tablespoon

filling

gelatine sheets	2 x 6 g (⅛ oz) (or 2 teaspoons powdered gelatine)
milk	200 ml (7 fl oz)
caster (superfine) sugar	115 g (4 oz/½ cup)
good-quality white chocolate	80 g (2¾ oz/½ cup) chopped
egg yolks	4, at room temperature, lightly beaten
cream (whipping)	250 ml (9 fl oz/1 cup), whipped to soft peaks

chocolate glaze

cream (whipping)	60 ml (2 fl oz/¼ cup)
good-quality dark chocolate	80 g (2¾ oz/½ cup) chopped
unsalted butter	10 g (¼ oz), cubed
liquid glucose	2 teaspoons

Preheat the oven to 190°C (375°F/Gas 5). Lightly grease a 20 cm (8 inch) spring-form cake tin and line the base.

To make the pastry, beat the butter with electric beaters until smooth and fluffy. Beat in the sugar and egg until combined. Sift in the combined flours and cocoa powder and stir until the dough comes together. Knead briefly on a lightly floured surface until smooth. Flatten into a disc, wrap in plastic wrap and refrigerate for 30 minutes.

Roll the pastry between two sheets of baking paper until about 8 mm (⅜ inch) thick, and trim to fit the base of the prepared tin. Ease the pastry into the tin, removing the paper, and lightly prick with a fork. Bake for 15 minutes, or until slightly firm to touch. Set aside to cool.

To make the filling, either soak the gelatine sheets in cold water for 5 minutes, or until soft, or put 2 tablespoons of water in a small bowl, sprinkle with the powdered gelatine and set aside for 2 minutes to sponge and swell. Heat the milk, sugar and chocolate in a saucepan until simmering. Stir until the sugar has dissolved and the chocolate has melted. Put the egg yolks in a bowl and whisk in the warm chocolate mixture. Return the mixture to a clean saucepan and stir over medium heat until it lightly coats the back of a spoon. Drain the gelatine sheets and squeeze out the excess water. Add the gelatine sheets or the sponged gelatine to the saucepan and stir until the gelatine has dissolved. Transfer to a bowl, place over a bowl of ice and beat until cold. Fold in the cream. Pour the mixture over the pastry and refrigerate overnight, or until set.

To make the chocolate glaze, put the cream, chocolate, butter and glucose in a saucepan and stir over low–medium heat until smooth. Allow the glaze to cool slightly until thickened.

Remove the tart from the tin and spoon the glaze over the top, allowing it to drip down the side. Use a metal spatula to smooth the glaze over the top of the tart. Set aside at room temperature for 1 hour, or until the glaze is set.

stem ginger cheesecake
with sauternes poached plums .... serves 8

THIS RECIPE OFFERS A SOPHISTICATED TWIST ON THE SMOOTH, RICH FLAVOURS OF TRADITIONAL CHEESECAKES.
IT IS STILL CREAMY, BUT HAS ADDED DEPTH FROM THE GINGER NUT BISCUIT BASE AND GINGER-TINGED FILLING.
THE PLUMS PROVIDE YET ANOTHER LAYER OF FLAVOUR AND TEXTURE — SWEET, FRUITY AND GOLDEN.

ginger nut biscuits (ginger snaps)	125 g (4½ oz)
unsalted butter	30 g (1 oz), melted
powdered gelatine	2 teaspoons
boiling water	60 ml (2 fl oz/¼ cup)
cream cheese	500 g (1 lb 2 oz/2 cups)
sweetened condensed milk	400 g (14 oz) tin
stem ginger in syrup	2 pieces, chopped, plus 60 ml (2 fl oz/¼ cup) syrup
plums	350 g (12 oz)
Sauternes	100 ml (3½ fl oz)
caster (superfine) sugar	2 tablespoons

Put the ginger nut biscuits in a food processor and process until they form fine crumbs. Transfer the crumbs to a bowl and combine with the melted butter. Spoon the mixture into a 20 cm (8 inch) spring-form cake tin, pressing firmly to make a base. Refrigerate for 30 minutes.

Dissolve the gelatine in the boiling water. Put the cream cheese, condensed milk, ginger, syrup and the gelatine mixture in a food processor and process until smooth. Pour over the chilled base and refrigerate for 3 hours.

Halve the plums, removing the stones. Combine the Sauternes and sugar in a saucepan and add the plums in a single layer. Gently poach the plums for 4 minutes, then set aside to cool.

Arrange the plums, cut side up, on top of the cheesecake and drizzle with the poaching liquid.

A knobbly, brown rhizome from a tropical plant, ginger may not have the beauty of saffron or rosewater, or the exotic charm of vanilla beans or cinnamon sticks, but it is just as indispensable in the kitchen as any of these. Its value lies not only in its lively and refreshing flavour and aroma, but also in its medicinal properties. Ginger is indigenous to Southeast Asia, where it is used extensively in both savoury and sweet dishes. However, it is hard to find a cuisine that doesn't make use of ginger. It is available fresh year-round, and is also sold dried, powdered, crystallized and preserved in syrup as stem ginger.

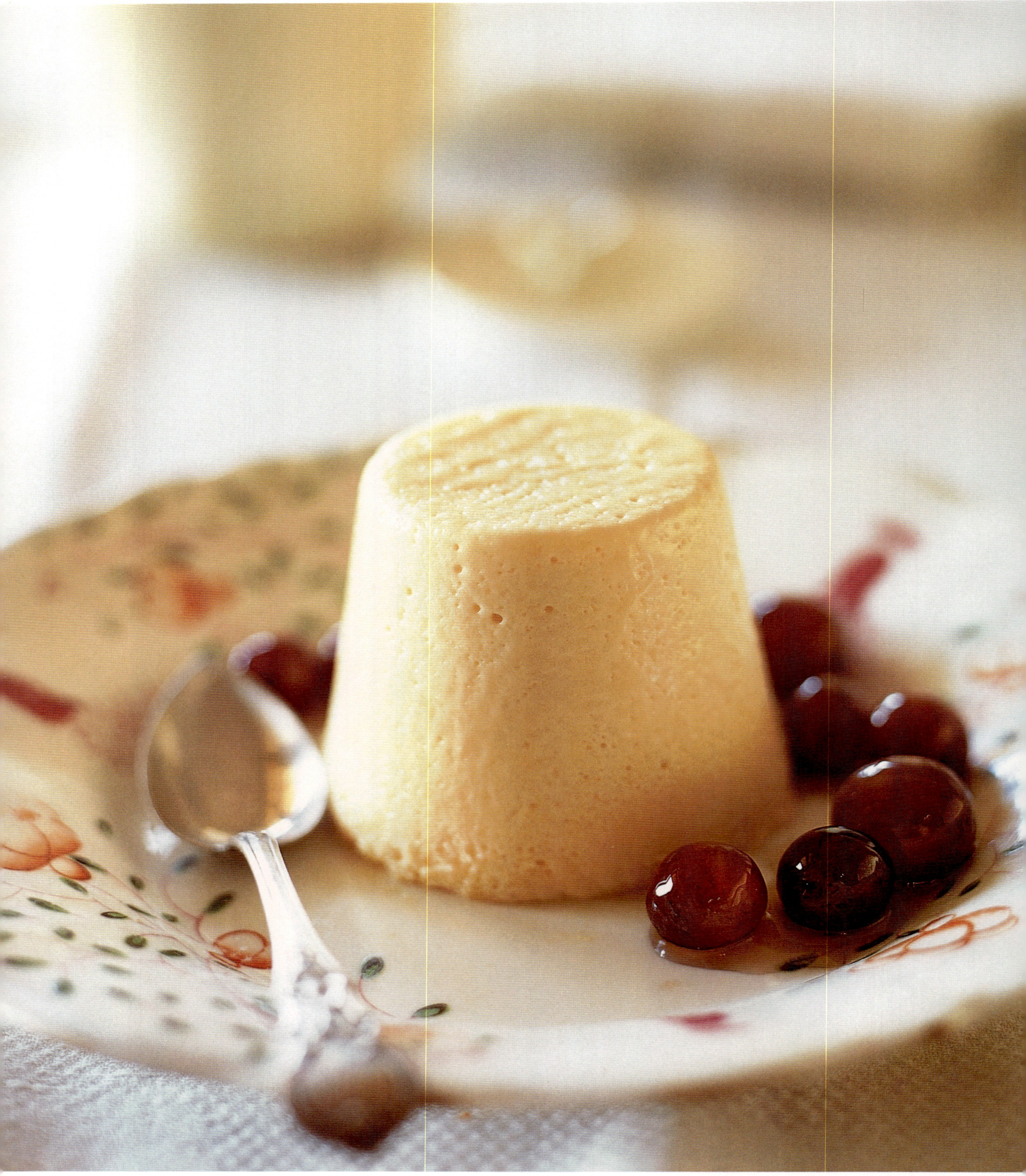

passionfruit mousse with red grape syrup .... serves 10

THE FLAVOURS AND COLOURS OF DESSERTS DON'T HAVE TO TURN SOMBRE JUST BECAUSE IT'S AUTUMN. THIS RECIPE COMBINES THE LIVELY TANG OF A PASSIONFRUIT-FLAVOURED MOUSSE WITH A SWEET RED GRAPE SYRUP. YOU WILL NEED ABOUT 20 FRESH PASSIONFRUIT OR 2 x 170 G (6 OZ) TINS OF PASSIONFRUIT PULP.

eggs	4, at room temperature, separated
caster (superfine) sugar	175 g (6 oz/³/4 cup), plus 2 tablespoons
passionfruit juice	185 ml (6 fl oz/³/4 cup), strained
powdered gelatine	2 tablespoons
hot water	60 ml (2 fl oz/¹/4 cup)
thickened (whipping) cream	300 ml (10¹/2 fl oz)
cherry brandy, such as Kirsch	60 ml (2 fl oz/¹/4 cup)
natural vanilla extract	1 teaspoon
seedless red grapes	200 g (7 oz)

Put the egg yolks and 175 g (6 oz/³/4 cup) of the sugar in a heatproof bowl and whisk with electric beaters until thick and pale. Stir in the passionfruit juice. Place the bowl over a saucepan of simmering water, making sure the base of the bowl doesn't touch the water. Stir for 6–8 minutes, or until the mixture is thick enough to coat the back of a wooden spoon.

Dissolve the gelatine in the hot water and add it to the passionfruit mixture. Set aside to cool.

Whip the cream until soft peaks form. In a separate bowl, beat the egg whites until soft peaks form. Gently fold the cream and egg whites through the passionfruit mixture. Pour into 10 x 125 ml (4 fl oz/¹/2 cup) moulds and refrigerate for 4 hours, or until set.

Meanwhile, put 125 ml (4 fl oz/¹/2 cup) of water, the cherry brandy, the remaining 2 tablespoons of sugar and the vanilla in a small saucepan. Stir over low heat until the sugar has dissolved, then increase the heat and simmer for 12 minutes. Remove from the heat, add the grapes and set aside to cool.

To serve, dip the base of each mould in hot water for 5 seconds and invert the mousse onto a plate. Accompany with the grapes and a little syrup.

Stir the passionfruit juice into the sugar and eggs.

Cook the custard gently until it coats the back of the spoon.

Divide the passionfruit mixture among the moulds.

corella pear tarte tatin.. serves 6

THIS DESSERT IS JUSTIFIABLY A CLASSIC — IT IS VERY EASY TO MAKE, AND LOOKS AND TASTES GREAT. CORELLA PEARS ARE SMALL WITH A PRETTY GREEN SKIN AND PINK BLUSH; THEIR FIRM, WHITE FLESH HAS A RICH LUSHNESS TO IT. OTHER GOOD VARIETIES TO USE ARE PACKHAM AND BEURRE BOSC.

unsalted butter	50 g (1¾ oz), chopped
raw caster (superfine) sugar	90 g (3¼ oz/heaped ⅓ cup)
corella pears	5
pecans	9
frozen puff pastry	2 sheets, thawed
cream or vanilla ice cream	to serve

Put the butter and sugar in a 20 cm (8 inch) tarte tatin tin or heavy-based frying pan with an ovenproof handle. Heat gently, without stirring, for 1 minute, or until the sugar has caramelized and turned golden brown. Don't worry if the butter separates at this stage. Remove from the heat.

Peel, halve and core the pears, leaving the stalks intact. Arrange the pears, cut side up, in a circle over the caramel, with the stalks towards the centre. Place one pear half in the centre and fill in the gaps with the pecans. Cover and cook the pears over low heat for 20 minutes, or until tender.

Preheat the oven to 190°C (375°F/Gas 5). Lay one sheet of pastry on top of the other and roll firmly and evenly so that they stick together and increase in size by 1–2 cm (½–¾ inch). Trim the pastry to a circle 2.5 cm (1 inch) larger than the upper rim of the tin and place over the pears. Gently push the edges of the pastry down between the pears and the tin.

Bake for 20 minutes, or until golden. Carefully drain the sauce from the tin into a small saucepan and simmer for 4–5 minutes, or until reduced and syrupy. Turn the tarte tartin out onto a serving plate and pour the reduced sauce over the top. Serve immediately with cream or vanilla ice cream.

Arrange the pears, cut side up, in the tin.

Lay the pastry over the pears and tuck the edge down the side.

winter

There are no half measures in winter; instead, there are layers upon layers of everything that is rich and satisfying. Gooey chocolate puddings come with a chocolate sauce, and chocolate, hazelnut and orange dessert cake is served with a blood orange sauce. The colours are deep and golden, the tastes and textures wonderfully warm, sweet and indulgent. Pity the brave person who decides to diet this winter! For, while it is true that apple and passionfruit crumble and almond and rosewater puddings with orange and date salad manage to avoid chocolate and cream — even the hedonists among us need the occasional change of pace — these light offerings are not the real focus of this chapter. Instead, most of the recipes here seem to have but one goal: to make sure you and your guests finish a meal truly and gloriously satisfied.

Many of the recipes are very simple to make — almost comforting, such is the emphasis on gently melting chocolate, slowly caramelizing apples in butter and sugar, steadily folding through whipped cream. Similarly, the bulk of the ingredients are reassuringly familiar — eggs, cream, flour, almonds, vanilla, and chocolate, lots of it. Chocolate is the unchallenged star of this chapter, so it's worth buying a good-quality block, particularly when it is the key flavouring in a recipe. Look for chocolate with at least 50 per cent cocoa liquor, and which does not contain vegetable fats.

Most of us are happy to have chocolate with pretty much anything, but there are a few standout combinations that are hard to surpass — chocolate with liqueurs, with nuts such as hazelnuts and almonds, with spices such as cinnamon, and with fruit such as oranges. Winter also sees the arrival of cumquats and blood oranges, both visually dramatic ways to signal the season. Try honey parfait with caramelized cumquats, or topping a favourite pudding with a hot blood orange and cardamom sauce. Don't forget, however, those old faithfuls apples and bananas, which also excel during the colder months — recipes include brioche with caramelized apples and crème anglaise, and banana fritters with butterscotch sauce. Like many of the desserts here featuring fruit, it's hard not to suspect that their primary purpose is to serve as a foil to a very good sauce: bananas with butterscotch, oranges with caramel, and strawberries with chocolate and liqueur.

brioche and butter pudding .... serves 8

IF THIS DOESN'T WARM YOU UP ON A COLD WINTER'S NIGHT, NOTHING WILL. BRIOCHE IS A LIGHT BUT RICH, BUTTERY BREAD; IF NOT AVAILABLE, TRY CRUSTY WHITE BREAD, CROISSANTS OR EVEN PANETTONE. TO MAKE YOUR OWN CINNAMON SUGAR, COMBINE TWO PARTS CASTER (SUPERFINE) SUGAR WITH ONE PART GROUND CINNAMON.

golden syrup or dark corn syrup	2 tablespoons
brioche or crusty white bread	10 x 2 cm (3/4 inch) thick slices
unsalted butter	40 g (1 1/2 oz), softened
apricot jam	90 g (3 1/4 oz/heaped 1/4 cup)
eggs	4, at room temperature
sugar	90 g (3 1/4 oz/heaped 1/3 cup)
milk	800 ml (28 fl oz)
natural vanilla extract	1 teaspoon
cinnamon sugar	1/2 teaspoon

caramel sauce

unsalted butter	90 g (3 1/4 oz), chopped
soft brown sugar	60 g (2 1/4 oz/1/3 cup)
golden syrup or dark corn syrup	2 tablespoons
cream (whipping)	250 ml (9 fl oz/1 cup)

Preheat the oven to 180°C (350°F/Gas 4) and lightly grease a 2.25 litre (79 fl oz/9 cup) capacity ovenproof dish. Drizzle the golden syrup into the dish.

Spread the brioche slices with the butter and apricot jam and arrange in layers in the prepared dish.

Whisk the eggs, sugar, milk and vanilla in a bowl until combined. Slowly pour the mixture over the brioche, allowing it to be absorbed gradually. Set aside for 10 minutes for some of the liquid to be absorbed into the brioche. Sprinkle with the cinnamon sugar and bake for 40 minutes, or until a knife comes out clean when inserted into the centre of the pudding.

Meanwhile, to make the caramel sauce, put the butter, brown sugar and golden syrup in a small saucepan and bring to the boil. Add the cream, reduce the heat and simmer for 3–4 minutes.

Serve the caramel sauce poured over the warm pudding.

Obtaining vanilla is a labour-intensive and involved process, which helps explain why it is such an expensive flavouring. The pollination of the climbing orchid vine from which vanilla is obtained is intricate, and occurs naturally only in its native Mexico. The resulting green beans are picked, dried and fermented. This causes them to shrivel, turn deep brown and acquire a light coating of white vanillin crystals, the source of the all-important flavour. Good-quality vanilla beans have a warm, caramel aroma and flavour, and should be soft, not hard and dry. Vanilla is also sold distilled into natural vanilla extract — beware of cheap imitations.

banana fritters
with butterscotch sauce

serves 4

IT'S EASY TO SEE WHY THIS FABULOUS DESSERT IS A CHILDHOOD FAVOURITE — MELTING BANANA IN A CRISPY, HOT CASING WITH SMOOTH, GOLDEN BUTTERSCOTCH SAUCE. THE WARM BANANA SMELLS WONDERFUL TOO, ADDING TO THE PLEASURE. YOU CAN STORE ANY LEFTOVER SAUCE IN THE REFRIGERATOR FOR UP TO 2 WEEKS.

butterscotch sauce

unsalted butter	60 g (2¼ oz)
golden syrup or dark corn syrup	115 g (4 oz/⅓ cup)
soft brown sugar	60 g (2¼ oz/⅓ cup)
caster (superfine) sugar	55 g (2 oz/¼ cup)
cream (whipping)	170 ml (5½ fl oz/⅔ cup)
natural vanilla extract	½ teaspoon

batter

self-raising flour	125 g (4½ oz/1 cup)
egg	1, at room temperature, beaten
soda water	185 ml (6 fl oz/¾ cup)
unsalted butter	20 g (¾ oz), melted

oil	for deep-frying
firm bananas	4
icing (confectioners') sugar	for dusting
ice cream	to serve

To make the butterscotch sauce, put the butter, golden syrup, brown sugar and caster sugar in a small saucepan. Stir over low heat for 2–3 minutes, or until the sugar has dissolved. Increase the heat a little and simmer for 3–5 minutes, taking care not to burn the sauce. Remove the pan from the heat and stir in the cream and vanilla.

To make the batter, sift the flour into a bowl and make a well in the centre. Add the egg and soda water and whisk until smooth. Whisk in the melted butter.

Fill a saucepan one-third full of oil and heat to 200°C (400°F), or until a cube of bread dropped into the oil browns in 5 seconds.

Cut each banana into thirds and add to the batter in batches. Use a spoon to coat the banana in the batter.

Using a slotted spoon, carefully lower the banana into the hot oil in batches. Cook each batch for 2–3 minutes, turning until the fritters are puffed and golden brown all over. Drain the fritters on paper towels.

Serve the fritters hot, dusted with icing sugar. Accompany with ice cream and the butterscotch sauce.

Melt the butter, sugars and golden syrup together.

Dip the pieces of banana into the batter in batches.

chocolate, almond and cardamom cake

THOUGH THIS CAKE COULD NOT BE EASIER TO MAKE, IT DOES NOT LACK FLAVOUR. GROUND CARDAMOM, LIKE ANY SPICE, CAN LOSE ITS AROMATIC QUALITIES OVER TIME, SO BUY FROM A SPECIALIST SPICE STORE OR GRIND YOUR OWN. CRÈME FRAÎCHE HAS A SLIGHTLY NUTTY, SHARP FLAVOUR, WHICH COMPLEMENTS THE SWEET CHOCOLATE.

good-quality dark chocolate	250 g (9 oz/1²/3 cups) chopped
unsalted butter	250 g (9 oz), chopped
natural vanilla extract	1 teaspoon
hot water	250 ml (9 fl oz/1 cup)
caster (superfine) sugar	175 g (6 oz/³/4 cup)
eggs	3, at room temperature, lightly beaten
self-raising flour	165 g (5³/4 oz/1¹/3 cups)
ground almonds	100 g (3¹/2 oz/1 cup)
ground cardamom	3 teaspoons
icing (confectioners') sugar	30 g (1 oz/¹/4 cup)
crème fraîche or whipped cream	to serve

Preheat the oven to 160°C (315°F/Gas 2–3). Grease a 24 cm (9¹/2 inch) spring-form cake tin.

Put the chocolate, butter, vanilla and hot water in a heatproof bowl. Sit the bowl over a saucepan of barely simmering water, making sure the base of the bowl doesn't touch the water. Heat gently until the chocolate has melted. Remove from the heat and stir in the caster sugar. Add the eggs and beat well to combine.

Combine the sifted flour, ground almonds and 2 teaspoons of the cardamom and fold through the chocolate mixture, beating well to combine. Pour the mixture into the prepared tin and bake for 40 minutes, or until a skewer inserted into the centre of the cake comes out almost clean. Set aside in the tin for 10 minutes, then turn out onto a wire rack to cool.

Combine the remaining cardamom with the icing sugar and dust over the cooled cake. Serve with crème fraîche or cream.

Add the dry ingredients to the chocolate mixture.

Beat well to combine the chocolate and dry ingredients.

Pour the mixture into a spring-form cake tin.

orange crème caramel . . . . serves 6

THE AIM HERE IS TO PRODUCE A SILKY SMOOTH CUSTARD WITH NO (OR AT LEAST FEW) BUBBLES IN IT. EASIER SAID THAN DONE, AND GENERALLY PRACTICE IS THE BEST SOLUTION. GET TO KNOW YOUR OVEN AND NOTE WHAT HAPPENS. HAVING THE OVEN TOO HOT OR COOKING FOR TOO LONG CAN LEAD TO ROGUE AIR BUBBLES FORMING.

oranges	4 small
milk	250 ml (9 fl oz/1 cup)
cream (whipping)	250 ml (9 fl oz/1 cup)
vanilla bean	1, split lengthways
eggs	3, at room temperature
egg yolks	2, at room temperature
caster (superfine) sugar	115 g (4 oz/1/2 cup)

caramel

caster (superfine) sugar	350 g (12 oz/11/2 cups)

Preheat the oven to 160°C (315°F/Gas 2–3) and half-fill a large roasting tin with water. Place the roasting tin in the oven.

Grate the zest of two of the oranges, then peel all the oranges, removing the rind and all the pith. Cut each orange into six slices, discarding any seeds, and place in a flat, heatproof dish.

To make the caramel, put the sugar and 185 ml (6 fl oz/3/4 cup) of water in a small saucepan over medium heat. Stir constantly for 5 minutes, or until the sugar has completely dissolved. Brush any undissolved sugar from the side of the saucepan with a wet pastry brush. When the sugar has dissolved, increase the heat and boil, without stirring, for 6–7 minutes, or until the mixture has turned golden brown.

Pour the caramel into the base of 6 x 185 ml (6 fl oz/3/4 cup) ovenproof ramekins, reserving about 125 ml (4 fl oz/1/2 cup) of the caramel. Quickly, but carefully, stir 1 tablespoon of water into the reserved caramel and pour over the sliced oranges. Cover and refrigerate the oranges.

Put the milk, cream, vanilla bean and orange zest in a saucepan. Slowly bring to the boil, then remove from the heat and set aside to infuse for 10 minutes. Beat the eggs, egg yolks and sugar in a bowl with electric beaters for 2–3 minutes, or until pale and creamy. Strain the milk mixture over the egg mixture and beat until smooth. Pour the mixture into the ramekins containing the caramel. Put the ramekins into the roasting tin of water and bake for 45 minutes, or until a knife inserted into the centre comes out clean. Cover the ramekins with foil if the surface is browning too quickly, making sure the foil doesn't touch the surface. Remove the ramekins from the roasting tin and set aside to cool, then cover and refrigerate for several hours, or overnight.

Remove the crème caramels and oranges from the refrigerator 30 minutes before serving. Unmould the crème caramels onto plates and serve with the oranges.

white chocolate torte . . . . serves 6–8

WHAT AN INGREDIENT LIST — EGGS, SUGAR, CHOCOLATE, FLOUR, CREAM, MORE CHOCOLATE AND MASCARPONE
CHEESE! THIS CAKE IS A VERY SIMPLE ONE TO PREPARE, BUT RICH. SERVE A SLICE WITH STRONG COFFEE AND
SOME FRESH WINTER FRUIT.

eggs	3, at room temperature
caster (superfine) sugar	80 g (2¾ oz/⅓ cup)
white chocolate	80 g (2¾ oz/½ cup) chopped, melted
plain (all-purpose) flour	60 g (2¼ oz/½ cup), sifted
white chocolate curls	to serve

topping

thickened (whipping) cream	150 ml (5 fl oz)
white chocolate	250 g (9 oz/1⅔ cups) chopped
mascarpone cheese	125 g (4½ oz/scant ⅔ cup)

Preheat the oven to 180°C (350°F/Gas 4) and grease a 20 cm (8 inch) spring-form cake tin.

Beat the eggs and sugar with electric beaters until thick and pale. Fold in the melted white chocolate and sifted flour. Pour into the prepared tin and bake for 20 minutes, or until a skewer inserted into the centre of the cake comes out clean. Set aside in the tin to cool completely.

To make the topping, put the cream and white chocolate in a saucepan. Stir constantly over low heat for 5–6 minutes, or until the chocolate has melted and the mixture is smooth. Remove from the heat and set aside to cool slightly. Stir the mascarpone into the chocolate mixture.

Remove the cake from the tin and use a spatula to spread the topping over the top and side. Refrigerate overnight, or until the topping is firm. Serve topped with the chocolate curls.

The process needed to transform the cacao bean (cocoa in English) into that smooth, delicious end result known as chocolate is long and complicated, and the block of chocolate, so ubiquitous now, was not perfected until the 1840s. The beans are fermented, dried and roasted, and the exposed nibs ground with water to make chocolate liquor. From this comes cocoa butter, as well as a paste that can be dried to make cocoa powder. It is cocoa butter, combined with ground beans and other ingredients such as sugar, that produces chocolate. White chocolate is made from cocoa butter and milk solids, although it differs from milk and dark chocolate in that it does not contain chocolate liquor.

honey parfait with
caramelized cumquats .... serves 6

GOLDEN CUMQUATS, LOOKING LIKE MINIATURE ORANGES, HAVE A FLAVOUR THAT IS BOTH SWEET AND TART AT THE SAME TIME. THE ENTIRE FRUIT IS EDIBLE, SO THERE IS NO NEED TO PEEL THEM FOR COOKING. THIS IS FORTUNATE, BECAUSE IT IS ACTUALLY THE SKIN THAT PROVIDES THE SWEETNESS, NOT THE FLESH.

honey	90 g (3¼ oz/¼ cup)
egg yolks	4, at room temperature
cream (whipping)	300 ml (10½ fl oz), whipped to soft peaks
orange liqueur, such as Grand Marnier	1 tablespoon
cumquats	500 g (1 lb 2 oz)
caster (superfine) sugar	350 g (12 oz/1½ cups)

Put the honey in a small saucepan and bring to the boil. Beat the egg yolks in a bowl until thick and pale, then add the honey in a slow stream, beating constantly. Gently fold in the cream and liqueur. Pour the mixture into 6 x 125 ml (4 fl oz/½ cup) freezer-proof moulds. Freeze for 4 hours, or until firm.

Wash the cumquats and prick the skins with a skewer. Place the cumquats in a large saucepan, cover with boiling water and simmer for 20 minutes. Strain the cumquats and reserve 500 ml (17 fl oz/2 cups) of the liquid. Return the liquid to the saucepan, add the sugar and stir over medium heat until the sugar has dissolved. Increase the heat and boil for 10 minutes. Add the cumquats and simmer for 20 minutes, or until the cumquats are soft and the skins are smooth and shiny. Remove from the heat and set aside to cool. Lift the cumquats out of the syrup, reserving the syrup.

To serve, dip the moulds in hot water for 5–10 seconds before inverting the parfait onto serving plates. Serve with the caramelized cumquats, with a little of the syrup spooned over the top.

Add the boiled honey to the egg yolks, beating constantly.

Prick the skins of the cumquats with a skewer.

Simmer the cumquats until the skins are smooth and shiny.

baked chocolate puddings with rich chocolate sauce .... serves 6

THESE PUDDINGS ONLY TAKE AROUND 10 MINUTES TO COOK AND SHOULD BE SERVED IMMEDIATELY SO THAT THEIR LUSCIOUS RUNNY CENTRES CAN BE FULLY APPRECIATED. TO ENSURE A SMOOTH DELIVERY TO THE TABLE, HAVE EVERYTHING ABSOLUTELY READY BEFORE YOU BEGIN.

cocoa powder	1½ tablespoons
good-quality dark chocolate	120 g (4¼ oz/heaped ¾ cup) chopped
unsalted butter	120 g (4¼ oz), softened
eggs	3, at room temperature
egg yolks	2, at room temperature
caster (superfine) sugar	55 g (2 oz/¼ cup)
plain (all-purpose) flour	90 g (3¼ oz/¾ cup)

chocolate sauce

good-quality dark chocolate	80 g (2¾ oz/½ cup) chopped
cream (whipping)	125 ml (4 fl oz/½ cup)

Preheat the oven to 180°C (350°F/Gas 4) and grease 6 x 125 ml (4 fl oz/½ cup) metal dariole moulds. Dust the moulds with the cocoa powder.

Put the chocolate in a small heatproof bowl over a small saucepan of simmering water, making sure the base of the bowl doesn't touch the water. Allow the chocolate to melt, then add the butter. When the butter has melted, stir to combine, then remove from the heat.

Beat the eggs, egg yolks and sugar in a large bowl with electric beaters until thick, creamy and pale in colour. Gently fold in the chocolate mixture. Sift in the flour and gently fold through.

Spoon the mixture into the prepared moulds, leaving about 1 cm (½ inch) at the top of the moulds to allow the puddings to rise. Bake for 10 minutes, or until the top is firm and risen.

Meanwhile, to make the chocolate sauce, put the chocolate and cream in a small heatproof bowl and melt over a small saucepan of simmering water, making sure the base of the bowl doesn't touch the water. Stir until combined.

To serve, run a knife around the moulds to loosen the puddings, then carefully turn out onto serving plates. Drizzle with the sauce and serve immediately.

Beat the sugar and eggs until thick and creamy.

Fold the melted chocolate into the sugar and egg mixture.

three ways with hot sauces

A SAUCE IS DEFINED AS A SPOONABLE CONCOCTION, AND THESE YUMMY SAUCES WILL CERTAINLY HAVE YOU AT THE READY WITH SPOON IN HAND. TRADITIONALLY, SAUCES ARE USED TO ENHANCE THE FLAVOURS OF THE FOODS THEY ACCOMPANY, BUT THE ONES GIVEN HERE DISTINGUISH THEMSELVES IN THEIR OWN RIGHT: THE FIRST VIBRANTLY COLOURED AND SWEET; THE NEXT RICH AND SMOOTH; AND THE THIRD GENTLY AROMATIC AND MELLOW. ALL ARE AN EASY WAY OF TRANSFORMING INGREDIENTS LIKE FRESH FRUIT AND ICE CREAM INTO A FABULOUS DESSERT.

blood orange and cardamom sauce

Grate the zest of 2 blood oranges and juice them both. Combine 250 ml (9 fl oz/1 cup) water with 250 g (9 oz) sugar in a saucepan and stir constantly over medium heat until the sugar has dissolved. Add the orange zest and juice and 5 lightly crushed cardamom pods. Bring to the boil, then reduce the heat to low and simmer for 10 minutes, or until the sauce is a little syrupy. Serve warm. This sauce is delicious poured over puddings, crepes, cakes or fresh fruit salad. Makes 310 ml (10¾ fl oz/1¼ cups).

chocolate and baileys sauce

Put 100 g (3½ oz/⅔ cup) chopped good-quality dark chocolate, 30 g (1 oz) unsalted butter, 60 ml (2 fl oz/¼ cup) Irish cream liqueur, such as Baileys, and 185 ml (6 fl oz/¾ cup) thickened (whipping) cream in a heatproof bowl. Place the bowl over a saucepan of barely simmering water, making sure the base of the bowl doesn't touch the water. Heat until the chocolate has melted. Remove from the heat and stir well to combine. This is great poured over strawberries, ice cream or cheesecakes. Makes 375 ml (13 fl oz/1½ cups).

cinnamon and pear sauce

Peel, core and chop 3 just under-ripe pears and place in a saucepan with 350 ml (12 fl oz) water, 225 g (8 oz/1 cup) caster (superfine) sugar, the juice of ½ lemon and 2 cinnamon sticks. Bring to the boil, then reduce the heat and simmer for 10 minutes, or until the pears are soft. Remove the cinnamon sticks. Purée the sauce in a blender until smooth. Serve warm. This sauce is great poured over ice cream, fresh fruit or puddings. Makes 750 ml (26 fl oz/3 cups).

blood orange and cardamom sauce

coconut rice pudding with spiced saffron apples

serves 4

THIS CREAMY DESSERT WITH ITS DELICATELY SCENTED APPLE TOPPING SHOULD CONVINCE ALL DOUBTERS OF THE MERITS OF RICE PUDDING. APPLES ARE NOT OFTEN PAIRED WITH COCONUT OR RICE, BUT INFUSING THEM WITH THE AROMATIC QUALITIES OF CINNAMON AND SAFFRON TRANSPORTS THEM FROM THE ORCHARD TO THE TROPICS.

short-grain rice	140 g (5 oz/²/₃ cup)
milk	250 ml (9 fl oz/1 cup)
light coconut cream	270 ml (9¹/₂ fl oz)
unsalted butter	20 g (³/₄ oz)
caster (superfine) sugar	2¹/₂ tablespoons

saffron apples

red apples	3 small
apple juice	185 ml (6 fl oz/³/₄ cup)
cinnamon stick	1
saffron threads	a pinch
soft brown sugar	50 g (1³/₄ oz/¹/₄ cup)

Put the rice, milk, coconut cream and 100 ml (3¹/₂ fl oz) of water in a heavy-based saucepan over low–medium heat. Bring to the boil, then reduce the heat and simmer, stirring often to prevent the rice from sticking, for 15–20 minutes, or until the mixture is creamy. Beat in the butter and sugar.

Meanwhile, to make the saffron apples, halve and core the apples, then cut into slices. Put the sliced apples, apple juice, cinnamon stick, saffron threads and brown sugar in a saucepan over low–medium heat. Bring to the boil, then reduce the heat and simmer for 8 minutes, or until the apple is soft.

Serve the rice pudding warm, topped with the saffron apples and their syrup.

Delicious raw or cooked, versatile and amenable to many other flavours, apples are for many the first choice among fruit. They have been cultivated for hundreds of years and exist in many thousands of varieties. It's easy to forget that these everyday companions are seasonal, with most varieties at their peak from autumn to winter. Good eating apples are sweet and often only slightly acidic. They are also perfect for use in pies and tarts as their high sugar content means they will hold their shape well. The more acidic, tart apples become soft when stewed or baked and are ideal for purées and crumbles.

apple galettes

AS WITH MANY CLASSIC TARTS, THE BEAUTY OF THIS DESSERT LIES IN ITS SIMPLICITY — WARM, PUFFED PASTRY, SWEET FRUIT AND CARAMELIZED, SLIGHTLY CRUNCHY TOPPING. MAKE YOUR OWN VANILLA SUGAR BY BURYING WHOLE BEANS IN A JAR OF SUGAR. SEAL WELL AND ALLOW 2 TO 3 WEEKS FOR THE VANILLA TO INFUSE THE SUGAR.

ground almonds	35 g (1 1/4 oz/1/3 cup)
unsalted butter	20 g (3/4 oz), melted
butter puff pastry	2 sheets, frozen
egg yolk	1, at room temperature, sieved
pink lady apple	1
green apple	1
apricot jam	2 tablespoons, warmed and sieved
vanilla sugar	1 tablespoon
thick (double/heavy) cream	to serve

Preheat the oven to 200°C (400°F/Gas 6).

Combine the ground almonds and melted butter in a small bowl. Place one sheet of frozen pastry on a sheet of baking paper and lay the second sheet of pastry on top. Cut the pastry into four squares, cutting through the two layers of pastry. (This may be easier when the pastry has thawed slightly, but not too soft.) Slide the baking paper and pastry onto a baking tray.

Brush the pastry squares with the sieved egg yolk. Divide the almond mixture among the pastry and spread in a thin layer, leaving the border free.

Thinly slice the apples and alternate the red and green apple slices on each pastry square. Brush with the apricot jam and sprinkle with the vanilla sugar.

Bake the galettes for 15 minutes, or until puffed and golden. Serve warm with thick cream.

Brush each square of pastry with sieved egg yolk.

Spread the almond mixture onto each pastry square.

Alternate the red and green apple slices.

chocolate, hazelnut and orange dessert cake with blood orange sauce .... serves 6–8

THIS IS A LOVELY MOIST CAKE, NICELY COMPLEMENTED BY THE CITRUS SAUCE. BLOOD ORANGES HAVE ONLY A SHORT SEASON, SO GRAB THEM WHEN YOU CAN. THEY ARE RICH, SWEET AND AROMATIC, WITH BOLD RED PIGMENTATION IN THE FLESH AND SKIN. YOU WILL NEED FOUR TO FIVE BLOOD ORANGES FOR THE SYRUP.

good-quality dark chocolate	200 g (7 oz/1⅓ cups) chopped
blanched hazelnuts	200 g (7 oz/1½ cups)
unsalted butter	200 g (7 oz), softened
raw caster (superfine) sugar	175 g (6 oz/¾ cup)
eggs	4, at room temperature, separated
espresso instant coffee granules	3 teaspoons
orange	1, zest finely grated
cornflour (cornstarch)	100 g (3½ oz/heaped ¾ cup)
icing (confectioners') sugar	for dusting
thick (double/heavy) cream	to serve

blood orange syrup

blood orange juice	250 ml (9 fl oz/1 cup), strained
caster (superfine) sugar	55 g (2 oz/¼ cup)
orange liqueur, such as Cointreau	1 teaspoon, optional

Preheat the oven to 170°C (325°F/Gas 3) and grease a 20 cm (8 inch) spring-form cake tin.

Put the chocolate in a heatproof bowl and place the bowl over a saucepan of simmering water, making sure the base of the bowl doesn't touch the water. Heat until melted.

Put the hazelnuts in a food processor and process until finely chopped. Cream the butter and caster sugar in a large bowl with electric beaters until pale and fluffy. Add the egg yolks, one at a time, beating well after each addition. Gently stir in the melted chocolate, coffee granules and orange zest. Mix in the cornflour and chopped hazelnuts.

Whisk the egg whites until soft peaks form. Using a large metal spoon, fold a scoop of egg whites into the chocolate mixture. Gently fold in the remaining egg whites. Spoon the mixture into the prepared tin and level the surface. Bake for 30 minutes, then cover loosely with foil and bake for another 40–45 minutes, or until a skewer inserted into the centre of the cake comes out clean. Don't be too concerned if the surface cracks.

Meanwhile, to make the blood orange syrup, pour the strained orange juice into a small saucepan and add the sugar. Stir over low heat until the sugar has dissolved. Bring to the boil, then reduce the heat and simmer for 10–12 minutes, or until reduced by half. Stir in the liqueur, if using, and set aside to cool slightly.

To serve, cut the warm cake into slices. Lightly dust with icing sugar, spoon over a little of the warm orange syrup and serve with thick cream.

Add the chopped hazelnuts to the cake mixture.

Simmer the blood orange juice and sugar together.

brioche with caramelized apples and crème anglaise

. . . . serves 6

THIS IS A FAIRLY INDULGENT DISH BUT IT IS TEMPTING TO SERVE IT FOR BREAKFAST, ONE DECADENT DAY. JUST FOCUS ON THE FRUIT AS THE HEALTHY BIT. CRÈME ANGLAISE NEEDS TO BE CLOSELY WATCHED DURING COOKING, AS IT CAN EASILY CURDLE IF IT GETS TOO HOT.

crème anglaise

egg yolks	4, at room temperature
caster (superfine) sugar	55 g (2 oz/$1/4$ cup)
milk	170 ml ($5^1/2$ fl oz/$2/3$ cup)
cream (whipping)	170 ml ($5^1/2$ fl oz/$2/3$ cup)
vanilla bean	1, split lengthways

caramelized apples

granny smith apples	3
caster (superfine) sugar	115 g (4 oz/$1/2$ cup)
unsalted butter	20 g ($3/4$ oz)

brioche	6 x 2 cm ($3/4$ inch) thick slices
cream (whipping)	185 ml (6 fl oz/$3/4$ cup)
eggs	2, at room temperature
orange liqueur, such as Cointreau	2 tablespoons
caster (superfine) sugar	2 teaspoons
unsalted butter	30 g (1 oz)
icing (confectioners') sugar	for dusting

To make the crème anglaise, beat the egg yolks and sugar until just combined. Heat the milk, cream and vanilla bean in a saucepan until almost boiling. Remove from the heat and remove the vanilla bean, scraping the seeds into the liquid. Pour the hot milk mixture onto the egg yolk mixture, mixing well.

Strain the mixture back into a clean saucepan. Stir constantly with a wooden spoon over low heat until the custard has thickened. Do not allow the custard to boil or it will curdle. Test the consistency by dipping the spoon into the custard and drawing your finger through it — it should leave a clean line. Pour the custard into a bowl, cover and refrigerate until cold.

To make the caramelized apples, peel and core the apples and cut each into eight wedges. Sprinkle some of the sugar over the base of a heavy-based frying pan and heat gently until the sugar has melted. Sprinkle the remaining sugar into the pan and stir until lightly golden. Add the butter and stir until melted. Add the apple and cook over high heat, gently stirring from time to time, for 10 minutes, or until the apple is well browned. Take care not to overcook the apple — it should still hold its shape. The sugar and butter may separate, but will come back together while the apple is cooking. Remove the pan from the heat and keep warm.

Cut each brioche slice into a 9 cm ($3^1/2$ inch) round. Combine the cream, eggs, liqueur and sugar in a bowl. Melt the butter in a large frying pan over medium heat. Dip the brioche into the egg mixture, allowing it to soak in slightly, then fry until golden brown on both sides. Remove from the pan and keep warm.

To serve, pour a portion of cold crème anglaise on a serving plate, top with a round of brioche and spoon the caramelized apple onto the brioche. Dust lightly with icing sugar.

Use a cookie cutter to cut rounds from the brioche slices.

Allow each brioche round to soak up some of the egg mixture.

pear and walnut frangipane tart .... serves 6–8

FRANGIPANE IS TRADITIONALLY MADE WITH ALMONDS, BUT THIS WALNUT VERSION WORKS PARTICULARLY WELL WITH PEARS. IT WILL RISE SLIGHTLY AS IT COOKS, SURROUNDING THE FRUIT AND HOLDING IT IN PLACE. FRANGIPANE GOES WITH A WHOLE ARRAY OF FRUIT, SO IS AN EXCELLENT BASIC RECIPE TO HAVE IN YOUR REPERTOIRE.

pastry

plain (all-purpose) flour	175 g (6 oz/1⅓ cups)
unsalted butter	90 g (3¼ oz), chilled and cubed
egg	1, at room temperature
iced water	2–3 tablespoons
lemon juice	3 teaspoons
pears	3
ground cinnamon	½ teaspoon
caster (superfine) sugar	2 tablespoons
vanilla bean	1, split lengthways
icing (confectioners') sugar	for dusting

walnut frangipane

unsalted butter	100 g (3½ oz), softened
caster (superfine) sugar	115 g (4 oz/½ cup)
natural vanilla extract	1 teaspoon
eggs	2, at room temperature
ground walnuts	150 g (5½ oz/1¼ cups)
plain (all-purpose) flour	30 g (1 oz/¼ cup)

To make the pastry, preheat the oven to 190°C (375°F/Gas 5). Lightly grease a 23 cm (9 inch) tart tin. Sift the flour and a pinch of salt into a bowl. Lightly rub the butter into the flour until the mixture resembles breadcrumbs. Beat the egg, half the water and the lemon juice together in a small bowl, then sprinkle evenly over the flour mixture. Stir with a flat-bladed knife to form a dough, adding the remaining water if necessary. Knead the dough a couple of times on a lightly floured surface. Flatten into a disc, wrap in plastic and refrigerate for 1 hour.

Peel, core and slice the pears. Put the pear, cinnamon and sugar in a saucepan. Scrape the seeds from the vanilla bean into the saucepan and add the pod. Add 60 ml (2 fl oz/¼ cup) of water and heat until simmering, then cook for 8 minutes, or until the pear is soft. Set aside.

To make the walnut frangipane, beat the butter and sugar until light and creamy. Add the vanilla and the eggs, one at a time, beating well after each addition. Fold in the ground walnuts and flour until combined.

Roll out the pastry between two sheets of baking paper to line the prepared tin. Carefully place the pastry in the tin, removing the baking paper, and trim any excess pastry. Lightly prick the base with a fork. Refrigerate for 10 minutes.

Line the pastry shell with a sheet of crumpled baking paper and pour in some baking beads or uncooked rice. Bake for 15 minutes, remove the paper and beads and return to the oven for another 5–8 minutes, or until slightly golden.

Spread the walnut frangipane into the pastry shell and arrange the pear slices on top. Bake for 30–35 minutes, or until the top is lightly browned and the frangipane is firm when tested with a skewer. Serve dusted with icing sugar.

Add a little water to help soften the pears.

Make sure the frangipane mixture is well combined.

chocolate and cinnamon
self-saucing puddings .... serves 4

THESE INDIVIDUAL PUDDINGS ARE A GREAT WAY TO END A MEAL, AND ALTHOUGH ALL THE WORK NEEDS TO BE DONE ON THE SPOT, THAT SHOULD ONLY TAKE ABOUT 30 MINUTES. THEN, JUST 40 MINUTES IN THE OVEN BEFORE YOU ARE SERVING UP SOME VERY GOOEY, VERY NICE, RICH PUDDINGS.

good-quality dark chocolate	50 g (1^3/4 oz/^{1}/3 cup) chopped
unsalted butter	60 g (2^1/4 oz), cubed
cocoa powder	2 tablespoons, sifted
milk	160 ml (5^1/4 fl oz)
self-raising flour	125 g (4^1/2 oz/1 cup)
caster (superfine) sugar	115 g (4 oz/^{1}/2 cup)
soft brown sugar	80 g (2^3/4 oz/^{1}/3 cup firmly packed)
egg	1, at room temperature, lightly beaten
thick (double/heavy) cream	to serve

cinnamon sauce

ground cinnamon	1^1/2 teaspoons
unsalted butter	50 g (1^3/4 oz), cubed
soft brown sugar	60 g (2^1/4 oz/^{1}/3 cup)
cocoa powder	30 g (1 oz/^{1}/4 cup), sifted

Preheat the oven to 180°C (350°F/Gas 4) and grease 4 x 250 ml (9 fl oz/1 cup) ovenproof dishes.

Combine the chocolate, butter, cocoa and milk in a saucepan. Stir over low heat until the chocolate has melted. Remove from the heat.

Sift the flour into a large bowl and stir in the sugars. Add to the chocolate mixture with the egg and mix well. Spoon the mixture into the prepared dishes, put on a baking tray and set aside.

To make the cinnamon sauce, put 375 ml (13 fl oz/1^1/2 cups) of water in a small saucepan. Add the cinnamon, butter, brown sugar and cocoa and stir over low heat until combined.

Pour the sauce onto the puddings over the back of a spoon. Bake for 40 minutes, or until firm. Turn out the puddings and serve with thick cream.

It seems every spice worth the name is difficult to harvest and has been prized and bitterly fought over in equal measure. Cinnamon is no exception. Its use dates back to ancient Egyptian times, where it was used as an embalming agent, and more recently battles have been fought for its control in its native Sri Lanka. As to harvesting, the inner bark is prised away from the tree *Cinnamomum zeylanicum*, cleaned, dried and sold as quills or sticks. Cassia bark is often sold as cinnamon, though it does not have the same fine qualities. Cinnamon is also available ground.

tiramisu ice cream .... serves 6–8

TIRAMISU MEANS 'PICK ME UP' IN ITALIAN AND THIS SUMPTUOUS ICE CREAM WILL DO JUST THAT. MARSALA IS A FORTIFIED WINE FROM SICILY, AGED FOR 2 TO 5 YEARS. IT HAS A RICH, SMOKY FLAVOUR AND A DARK AMBER COLOUR. LOOK FOR MARSALA FROM ITALY.

milk	250 ml (9 fl oz/1 cup)
vanilla bean	1, split lengthways
egg yolks	4, at room temperature
caster (superfine) sugar	150 g (5½ oz/⅔ cup)
instant coffee granules	20 g (¾ oz/⅓ cup)
sweet Marsala	80 ml (2½ fl oz/⅓ cup)
coffee liqueur	2 tablespoons
boiling water	125 ml (4 fl oz/½ cup)
thickened (whipping) cream	310 ml (10¾ fl oz/1¼ cups)
savoiardi (lady fingers)	6

Pour the milk into a saucepan. Scrape the seeds from the vanilla bean into the pan and add the pod. Heat slowly for 4–5 minutes, or until just below boiling point. Discard the vanilla pod. Beat the egg yolks and sugar with electric beaters until pale and frothy. Gradually pour the hot milk mixture over the egg mixture and beat until smooth. Return the mixture to the saucepan and stir constantly over low heat for 6–8 minutes, or until the custard has thickened and coats the back of a spoon.

Remove the pan from the heat. Strain the custard and divide it between two freezer-proof bowls. Dissolve half the coffee granules in one bowl and stir the Marsala into the other. Refrigerate both bowls of custard for 30 minutes.

Combine the remaining coffee granules, the coffee liqueur and boiling water in a small bowl. Refrigerate until required.

Whip the cream until soft peaks form. Fold half the cream through the coffee custard and half through the Marsala custard. Transfer the bowls to the freezer. When the ice cream starts to set, whisk well with electric beaters to break up the ice crystals. Return to the freezer until the ice cream is firm again, then beat well.

Line the base and the two long sides of an 8 x 17 cm (3¼ x 6½ inch), 6 cm (2½ inch) deep loaf (bar) tin with foil and brush with water. Spoon the coffee ice cream into the tin, levelling the surface. Dip both sides of the savoiardi in the chilled coffee liqueur mixture and arrange over the coffee ice cream in a tight layer, trimming to fit and gently pressing them down. Spoon the Marsala ice cream over the top and level the surface. Cover the tin with foil and freeze until set. Lift out of the tin, remove the foil and cut into slices to serve.

Alternatively, to prepare the ice cream in an ice-cream machine, churn the coffee custard until partly set, then spoon into the tin, top with the coffee-soaked savoiardi and freeze while you churn the Marsala custard.

Soak the savoiardi in the coffee liqueur mixture.

Cut the savoiardi to fit snugly in the tin.

the perfect soufflé

Soufflés can be sweet or savoury and are held up by beaten egg whites and hot air. Technically, soufflés are always hot, although iced or cold mousses are sometimes referred to as soufflés. A sweet soufflé is based on a custard or fruit purée base, to which melted chocolate, nuts, fruit and liqueur can be added. Once a soufflé mixture is made, it must be baked immediately and then served immediately.

To make the perfect chocolate soufflé, preheat the oven to 200°C (400°F/Gas 6) and put a baking tray into the oven to preheat. Wrap a double layer of baking paper around 6 x 250 ml (9 fl oz/1 cup) ramekins to come 3 cm (1¼ inches) above the rim and secure with string. This encourages the soufflé to rise well. Brush the insides of the ramekins with melted butter and sprinkle with caster (superfine) sugar, shaking to coat evenly and tipping out any excess. This layer of butter and sugar helps the soufflé to grip the sides and rise as it cooks.

Put 175 g (6 oz/1¼ cups) chopped good-quality dark chocolate in a large heatproof bowl. Place over a saucepan of simmering water, making sure the base of the bowl doesn't touch the water. Stir until the chocolate is melted and smooth, then remove the bowl from the saucepan. Stir 5 lightly beaten egg yolks and 60 g (2¼ oz/¼ cup) caster (superfine) sugar into the chocolate. Beat 7 egg whites until firm peaks form. Gently fold one-third of the egg whites into the chocolate mixture to loosen it. Then, using a metal spoon, fold in the remaining egg whites until just combined. Spoon the mixture into the prepared ramekins and run your thumb or a blunt knife around the inside rim of the dish and the edge of the mixture. This ridge helps the soufflé to rise evenly. Place the ramekins on the preheated baking tray and bake for 12–15 minutes, or until well risen and just set. Do not open the oven door while the soufflés are baking. Cut the string and remove the paper collars. Serve immediately, lightly dusted with sifted icing (confectioners') sugar. Makes 6.

nashi pear and rhubarb meringue tart

. . . . serves 6

MOST CHILDREN BLANCH AT RHUBARB. PERHAPS BECAUSE IT LOOKS LIKE A VEGETABLE — AND IS IN FACT BOTANICALLY CLASSIFIED AS SUCH. BUT WITH MATURITY COMES A NEW-FOUND APPRECIATION OF THE TENDER PINK STALKS — PARTICULARLY WHEN COOKED WITH JUICY NASHI PEAR AND SWEET MERINGUE.

pastry

unsalted butter	60 g (2 1/4 oz), chilled and cubed
plain (all-purpose) flour	125 g (4 1/2 oz/1 cup), sifted
caster (superfine) sugar	2 tablespoons
salt	1/2 teaspoon
iced water	1 tablespoon
egg yolks	2, at room temperature
natural vanilla extract	1/4 teaspoon

filling

nashi pears	2
rhubarb	5 stalks (about 410 g/14 1/2 oz)
caster (superfine) sugar	60 g (2 1/4 oz/1/4 cup)
vanilla bean	1, split lengthways
cornflour (cornstarch)	3 teaspoons

meringue

egg whites	3, at room temperature
caster (superfine) sugar	115 g (4 oz/1/2 cup)
icing (confectioners') sugar	for dusting

To make the pastry, preheat the oven to 180°C (350°F/Gas 4). Lightly grease a 22 cm (8 1/2 inch), 2 cm (3/4 inch) deep loose-based fluted tart tin. Rub the butter and flour together in a bowl until the mixture resembles breadcrumbs. Combine the sugar, salt, water, egg yolks and vanilla in a separate bowl, then blend into the flour mixture using a flat-bladed knife. Briefly knead the dough on a lightly floured surface until smooth. Flatten into a disc, wrap in plastic and refrigerate for 30 minutes.

Meanwhile, to make the filling, peel, core and cut the pears into 2 cm (3/4 inch) pieces. Trim and cut the rhubarb stalks into 4 cm (1 1/2 inch) lengths. Put the pear, sugar and 125 ml (4 fl oz/1/2 cup) of water in a saucepan. Scrape the seeds from the vanilla bean into the saucepan and add the pod. Bring to the boil, then stir, reduce the heat and simmer over low–medium heat for 5 minutes. Add the rhubarb and simmer for 10 minutes, or until the pear and rhubarb are soft. Stir 1 tablespoon of water into the cornflour until smooth, stir into the rhubarb mixture and cook until thickened. Set aside to cool. Discard the vanilla pod.

Roll out the pastry between two sheets of baking paper to line the prepared tin. Carefully place the pastry in the tin, removing the baking paper, and trim any excess pastry. Lightly prick the base with a fork. Refrigerate for 15 minutes.

Line the pastry shell with a sheet of crumpled baking paper and pour in some baking beads or uncooked rice. Bake for 15 minutes, remove the paper and beads and return to the oven for another 8 minutes. Set the pastry aside to cool. Increase the oven to 200°C (400°F/Gas 6).

To make the meringue, beat the egg whites with electric beaters until soft peaks form. Add the caster sugar, 1 tablespoon at a time, beating well after each addition until the sugar has dissolved. Continue beating and adding sugar until the meringue is thick and glossy. Spoon the filling into the pastry case, then spoon the meringue on top of the filling and dust with icing sugar. Bake for 8 minutes, or until lightly browned. Serve at room temperature.

Cut the trimmed rhubarb stalks into short lengths.

Use the back of a spoon to make peaks in the meringue.

apple and passionfruit crumble............................. serves 4–6

THERE ARE COUNTLESS VERSIONS OF THE FRUIT CRUMBLE BUT ALL RELY ON THE WINNING FORMULA OF SWEETENED FRUIT COVERED BY A GOLDEN TOPPING OF FLOUR, SUGAR AND BUTTER. HERE, PASSIONFRUIT AND SHREDDED COCONUT ADD A LITTLE COMPLEXITY TO THE BASIC FLAVOURS.

passionfruit	4
green apples	4
caster (superfine) sugar	55 g (2 oz/¼ cup), plus 80 g (2¾ oz/⅓ cup)
shredded coconut	60 g (2¼ oz/1 cup)
plain (all-purpose) flour	90 g (3¼ oz/¾ cup)
unsalted butter	80 g (2¾ oz), softened

Preheat the oven to 180°C (350°F/Gas 4) and grease a 1 litre (35 fl oz/4 cup) ovenproof dish.

Sieve the passionfruit, discarding the pulp, and place the juice in a bowl. Peel, core and thinly slice the apples and add to the passionfruit juice, along with the 55 g (2 oz/¼ cup) of sugar. Mix well, then transfer the mixture to the prepared dish.

Combine the shredded coconut, flour, extra sugar and butter in a bowl and rub together until the mixture has a crumble texture. Pile on top of the apple mixture.

Bake the crumble for 25–30 minutes, or until the topping is crisp and golden.

Make sure you squeeze out as much juice as possible.

Peel the apples and cut out all the cores.

Use your fingertips to rub the butter into the dry ingredients.

chocolate orange pots... serves 8

ANYTHING THAT CONTAINS CREAM AND CHOCOLATE AND NOT MUCH ELSE IS GOING TO BE RICH. AND WHILE THE ZEST OF ONE ORANGE WILL NOT DO MUCH TO ALTER THAT, ITS CLEAN, PERFUMED QUALITIES ARE AN ESSENTIAL PART OF THIS DISH. WASH AND DRY THE ORANGE BEFORE GRATING IT, TAKING CARE TO AVOID THE WHITE PITH.

thickened (whipping) cream	500 ml (17 fl oz/2 cups)
dark chocolate	250 g (9 oz/1²/₃ cups) chopped
powdered gelatine	2 teaspoons
egg yolks	6, at room temperature
orange	1, zest finely grated

Heat the cream in a small saucepan until it is just coming to the boil. Add the chocolate and stir over low heat until the chocolate has melted and the mixture is well combined.

Put 60 ml (2 fl oz/¹/₄ cup) of water in a small bowl and sprinkle with the gelatine. Leave the gelatine to sponge and swell. Stir the gelatine mixture into the hot chocolate mixture.

Beat the egg yolks with electric beaters for 3 minutes, or until thick and pale. Whisk a little of the hot chocolate mixture into the yolks, then pour the yolk mixture onto the remaining chocolate mixture, whisking continuously. Stir in the orange zest.

Divide the mixture among 8 x 125 ml (4 fl oz/¹/₂ cup) ramekins and refrigerate overnight to set. Serve the chocolate pots topped with extra orange zest, if desired.

Originating in China, oranges are now a mainstay of many people's daily diet the world over. Oranges have come far from their early days, and can be classified along the following lines: blood (vibrant colour, rich and sweet); sweet (good juice, some seeds); navel (easy to peel, full of flavour and nearly always seedless); and bitter Seville (aromatic skin and tart flavour; used in marmalade and liqueurs, and to make orange flower water). When buying, choose oranges that feel heavy and have tight skin. The skin of most commercially available oranges is coated with a wax polish. If you are using the zest, scrub the fruit very well first or, better still, buy organic unpolished oranges.

almond and rosewater puddings with orange and date salad . . . . serves 4

THESE PRETTY PUDDINGS CONTAIN ALMOND AROMA, WHICH IS AVAILABLE FROM SOME DELICATESSENS. IT LOOKS SIMILAR TO LIP BALM AND COMES IN A SIMILAR TYPE OF CONTAINER. IT IS PREFERABLE TO ALMOND EXTRACT; HOWEVER, 1/4 TEASPOON OF ALMOND EXTRACT CAN BE USED SUCCESSFULLY, IF NECESSARY.

powdered gelatine	3 teaspoons
milk	500 ml (17 fl oz/2 cups)
caster (superfine) sugar	2 tablespoons
bitter almond aroma	1/2 teaspoon
rosewater	1 teaspoon
oranges	2
fresh dates	8, pitted and roughly chopped

Put 60 ml (2 fl oz/1/4 cup) of water in a small bowl and sprinkle with the gelatine. Leave the gelatine to sponge and swell. Stir the milk and sugar in a small saucepan over medium heat until the sugar has dissolved. When the milk reaches lukewarm, remove the saucepan from the heat. Continue stirring while you add the gelatine mixture and stir until it has dissolved into the warm milk. Strain into a bowl, then stir in the almond aroma and rosewater.

Pour the mixture into 4 x 125 ml (4 fl oz/1/2 cup) dariole moulds and refrigerate for at least 3 hours, or until firm.

Remove the skin and pith from the oranges with a sharp knife. Holding the oranges over a bowl, remove the segments by slicing in between the membrane. Remove any seeds. Add the segments to the bowl with the juice. Squeeze any remaining juice from the orange skeletons. Add the chopped dates to the bowl and toss to combine.

To serve, wrap the dariole moulds in a hot, clean dish cloth and invert the puddings onto plates. Accompany the puddings with the orange and date salad.

Strain the warm milk and gelatine mixture into a bowl.

Peel the orange, removing all of the white pith.

Slice in between the membrane, avoiding any white pith.

ricotta, orange and walnut cake .... serves 6–8

THIS CAKE SHOWS JUST HOW MANY FLAVOURS ORANGES CAN COMPLEMENT — NUTS, RICOTTA AND COCOA. AS SUCH, IT NEEDS NO DRESSING UP. BUY THE DRY BULK RICOTTA AVAILABLE FROM DELICATESSENS FOR THIS CAKE; THE SMOOTH RICOTTA SOLD IN PRE-PACKAGED TUBS IS NOT SUITABLE.

walnut halves	150 g (5½ oz/1½ cups)
unsalted butter	150 g (5½ oz), softened
caster (superfine) sugar	150 g (5½ oz/⅔ cup)
eggs	5, at room temperature, separated
orange	1 large, zest finely grated
lemon juice	1 teaspoon
ricotta cheese	200 g (7 oz/heaped ¾ cup)
plain (all-purpose) flour	60 g (2¼ oz/½ cup)
dark cocoa powder	for dusting

candied orange zest

orange	1 large
orange juice	250 ml (9 fl oz/1 cup)
caster (superfine) sugar	115 g (4 oz/½ cup)

Preheat the oven to 200°C (400°F/Gas 6) and grease a 22 cm (8½ inch) spring-form cake tin.

Spread the walnuts on a baking tray and toast for 5 minutes. Use a sharp knife to roughly chop two-thirds of the walnuts. Set aside. Finely chop the remaining walnuts in a food processor and use to coat the inside of the prepared tin in a thick layer. Reduce the oven to 190°C (375°F/Gas 5).

Cream the butter and 90 g (3¼ oz/heaped ⅓ cup) of the sugar in a large bowl with electric beaters until pale and fluffy. Add the egg yolks, orange zest, lemon juice, ricotta, flour and reserved walnuts and mix gently until well combined.

Whisk the egg whites in a large bowl until soft peaks form. Gradually add the remaining sugar and whisk until stiff. Using a metal spoon, fold a large scoop of the egg white mixture into the ricotta mixture. Carefully fold in the remaining egg white mixture. Spoon into the prepared tin and level the surface. Bake for 35–40 minutes, or until the cake is set and the surface is golden. Cool in the tin for 15 minutes before turning out.

Meanwhile, to make the candied orange zest, carefully peel the orange using a sharp paring knife, discarding all the pith. Cut the zest into long strips, 3 mm (⅛ inch) wide. Place the zest in a bowl and cover with boiling water. Set aside to soak for 3–4 minutes, then drain and dry on paper towels. Stir the orange juice and sugar in a small saucepan until the sugar has dissolved. Bring to the boil, then add the orange zest and simmer for 5 minutes. Remove the zest with tongs and spread on a plate to cool.

To serve, dust the centre of the cake with cocoa, leaving 5 cm (2 inches) of the rim uncovered. Arrange the orange zest around the rim and serve the cake in slices.

Thinly slice the orange zest into long strips.

Simmer the zest in the sugar syrup for 5 minutes.

index

Published by Murdoch Books Pty Limited.

Murdoch Books Australia
Pier 8/9, 23 Hickson Road, Millers Point NSW 2000
Phone: +61 (0)2 8220 2000 Fax: +61 (0)2 8220 2558

Murdoch Books UK Limited
Erico House, 6th Floor North, 93–99 Upper Richmond Road
Putney, London SW15 2TG
Phone: + 44 (0) 20 8785 5995 Fax: + 44 (0) 20 8785 5985

Chief Executive: Juliet Rogers
Publisher: Kay Scarlett

Design concept and art direction: Vivien Valk
Designer: Annette Fitzgerald
Project manager: Paul McNally
Editor: Justine Harding
Text: Margaret Malone
Food editor: Katy Holder
Recipes: Lee Currie, Ross Dobson, Michelle Earl, Jo Glynn, Katy Holder,
Kathy Knudsen, Angela Nahas, Fiona Roberts, Mandy Sinclair, Abi Ulgiati
Photographer: Alan Benson
Stylist: Mary Harris
Food preparation: Jo Glynn
Production: Adele Troeger

National Library of Australia Cataloguing-in-Publication Data:
Cooking desserts.
Includes index.
ISBN 1 74045 523 1
1. Desserts.
641.86

Printed by Toppan Printing Hong Kong Co. Ltd. in 2005. PRINTED IN CHINA.

IMPORTANT: Those who might be at risk from the effects of salmonella poisoning (the elderly, pregnant women,
young children and those suffering from immune deficiency diseases) should consult their doctor with any
concerns about eating raw eggs.

CONVERSION GUIDE: You may find cooking times vary depending on the oven you are using. For fan-forced
ovens, as a general rule, set the oven temperature to 20°C (35°F) lower than indicated in the recipe. We have used
20 ml (4 teaspoon) tablespoon measures. If you are using a 15 ml (3 teaspoon) tablespoon, for most recipes the
difference will not be noticeable. However, for recipes using baking powder, gelatine, bicarbonate of soda (baking
soda), small amounts of flour and cornflour (cornstarch), add an extra teaspoon for each tablespoon specified.